The Reds Take a City

The Reds Take a City

The Communist Occupation of Seoul

with Eyewitness Accounts

By John W. Riley, Jr., and Wilbur Schramm

Narratives translated by Hugh Heung-wu Cynn

Rutgers University Press

New Brunswick, New Jersey

Manufactured in the United States of America

Foreword

What have we learned from the attempted Communist aggression in Korea?

The forces which reached into South Korea on June 25, 1950, were not only military and para-military forces, they were the total forces of a planned society. They decreed who could eat and who must starve, who could continue at his job and who must be enslaved, who could speak to what effect and who must parrot such thoughts. They touched every man, woman, and child in the conquered but unsubdued areas of South Korea. The experiences of these people as told and interpreted in the following pages give us an understanding of this all-powerful aspect of Communist aggression. It is important news for every American who wants to know better the design, the strengths, and the pliabilities of that against which the United Nations took up arms.

What happened in South Korea may not happen in exactly the same way in any other country. Many local and perhaps unique forces were at work to make the events of June to September, 1950, in certain ways peculiar to Korea. On the other hand there is a disturbing resemblance between what happened in South Korea in 1950 and what happened earlier in North Korea and in the European satellites. As the authors of this book point out, the model of the Communist blueprint for Seoul was Pyongyang, Prague, Bucharest, and Moscow.

Here, then, is the lesson in Communist intentions.

intentions which are being consistently planned for execution in every home—in city and on farm—around the world. In your home, too!

In the late fall of 1950, the United States Air Force assembled a team of experts on human problems. They were asked to begin the research which would attempt to assay the shape of Communist activities as these had been imposed upon the Korean people. The sudden attack from the north had rolled south of Seoul to Taejon within about two weeks. Out of a million and a half residents in Seoul, less than a hundred thousand had been able to flee ahead of the Red armies in their first drive southward. It was the social problems of these millions of Koreans trapped by the Reds which claimed the primary interest of the Air Force team.

Later in the fall of this same year, after the Communists had been driven northward out of Seoul, the experts appointed by the Air Force talked with and lived among these people. They made use of the resources of the national ministries and the city government. They conducted more than sixty detailed unstructured interviews with officials who, having remained in the city during the occupation, had been able expertly to observe events in their own fields. They had more than fifty long interviews with citizens of Seoul, representative of every walk of life, and more than thirteen hundred briefer interviews with refugees. They drew upon certain documentary sources, notably official reports made available by the ministries, reports of interrogations of prisoners of war (the Advanced Allied Translator and Interpreter Section) and a few captured documents from North Korea which shed light upon the Communist occupation plans. Finally, it should be noted that members of the team had the advice and assistance, during the entire period of their Korean stay, of twenty-five of the most eminent social scientists of Korea.

The authors of this volume were two members of the Air Force team: Dean Wilbur Schramm of the University of Illinois, a communications specialist, and Professor John W. Riley, Jr., a sociologist of Rutgers University. The personal and professional insights of these two men have been combined to describe the character and structure of the three months of Communist rule in Seoul, Korea. They have drawn upon portions of their reports to the Air Force, but the responsibility for their writing here must justly be credited to them alone.

Although the reading burden of scientific terminology and specialized writing has been lifted, the story is unaltered. It is not more circumscribed, nor is it taken out of context or oversimplified. Here may be seen people not unlike ourselves meeting personal problems of life and death. The canvas is spread to show the whole arena in which the people of Seoul suffered.

Included throughout are translations of narratives written by eminent Koreans who tell of their personal experiences during the ninety days of Red rule in the South. First published in Korea they have been faithfully translated by a Korean scholar now studying and working in the United States.

This is not a book to be read through at one sittting, extraordinary as such advice may sound, for the story is too provocative. Put it down after each chapter and think of the three months capsuled here. Think of three days in the life of any of these Korean men and women

—or of their compatriots whose life they represent for you. Put this book down occasionally and think of the three minutes, the three seconds, which meant life to the one who is telling his story and, so often, death to others. Reflect well upon the bitterness, the indignity and the inhumanity of the Communist leaders of aggression and their misled followers.

FREDERICK W. WILLIAMS

Maxwell Air Force Base, Alabama

Acknowledgments

Acknowledgment is hereby made to the Soodo and Eul Yu publishing companies of Seoul for their implied permission to reproduce in English parts of two volumes published by them. Communication with them was broken after the reoccupation of Seoul early in 1951.

Grateful acknowledgment is also made to the Human Resources Research Institute, and in particular to its Director, Dr. Raymond Bowers, to Dr. Frederick W. Williams, Professor John Pelzel, Colonel George Croker, Major Clarence Weems, to the score of Korean social scientists who were attached to the Air Force Research Mission, and to the many others who directly or indirectly contributed to the compilation of these materials.

Translator's Note

What has occurred and is occurring in Korea is an epitome of the world struggle between Communism and Democracy of the twentieth century. In Korea's long history of 4,283 years she has never experienced what she is experiencing now.

She is truly divided, territorially and economically. Her division has not been caused by an internal dissension, but by an inadvertency of her best friend, which is being exploited by an imperialistic neighbor. The weapons used by this neo-imperialist are ideological and military. The Communists are destroying humanity wherever they go in the name of saving humanity.

The experiences described in the pages of this book will create horrors in the mind of the readers, but it is to be remembered that these are the accounts of those who have successfully escaped the worst and final horrors. There are tens of thousands whose fate it was not to be able to escape, and whose bodies have been found in the mass-grave trenches. It is also to be remembered that there are those who are supposed to be living somewhere in northern Korea or Manchuria as captives—the civilian doctors, lawyers, teachers, religious leaders, American, British and French missionaries, foreign diplomats and prelates and army personnel. This is the foreshadow of what may come to other countries and peoples unless imperialistic Communism is driven out beyond the pale of human society.

HUGH HEUNG-WU CYNN

New York, New York
4 July 1951

Contents

The Reds
Take a City

The Reds Move into South Korea

Not long after the Japanese surrender a short but vital section of the iron curtain was lowered across the peninsular country that is Korea. It marked the boundary for the two postwar occupational powers—the United States and Russia. It was not an unusual arrangement. The Russians had insisted upon similar boundaries elsewhere. In Korea it was the 38th parallel. Then for five years the Reds worked undisturbed in the North.

Although this "line," which had been of interest only to geographers and map-makers, gradually took on political significance, no crisis seemed imminent. The United States forces in South Korea had been largely withdrawn, and the Republic of South Korea had been established without benefit of approval from the North. United Nations' efforts in the direction of a unified Korea repeatedly had been rebuffed, and Russia's unwillingness to cooperate on matters of Korean rehabilitation promised to continue indefinitely. Unlike Vienna, where some semblance of cooperative government has been maintained, and more like Berlin which serves as the knife edge separating eastern and western Germany, Korea, "the land of the morning calm," had become an uneasy "border" state.

The summer solstice of 1950 saw the rice paddies dotted with workers. Seoul—the political and industrial heart of South Korea—was attempting to order its affairs, sometimes arbitrarily but more often in a democratic spirit. Then it happened. On June 25 the ominous news was flashed to Seoul from the parallel: North Korean military forces had crossed the "line" and were moving South.

At first it sounded to the people of Seoul like a border clash, then like a more serious matter but one which the army of South Korea could handle satisfactorily. All mobile units of the R.O.K. army were rushed north. Trucks and requisitioned automobiles picked up the scattered semblance of an army. There was a series of sharp clashes. Then, while the people of Seoul waited for news, the gunfire rolled ever nearer across the mountains. Surprised and confused, the city soon saw the remnants of the R.O.K. forces begin to stream south through its streets. They had been outgunned and outmanned, with no equipment to oppose the Russian tanks which had come in the vanguard of the invasion army. On June 28, 1950, only three days after the invasion, the tanks and trucks of the North Korean People's army rumbled triumphantly into Seoul.

And they came to stay. This was no raid, it was a meticulously prepared, well-thought-out campaign. They expected complete military victory by July 15, and doubtless they would have achieved it had not the United Nations intervened. One of the carefully prepared Communist elections was to be held and a new national government was to be established in Seoul. Victory and unification were to be celebrated by a mammoth spectacle in Seoul during the month of September. Plans for these events progressed, although with postponements, to the very day of the Inchon landings.

The actions of the Communists in Seoul during the ninety days between their triumphal entry on June 28 and their hasty withdrawal on September 28 can hardly be interpreted, therefore, as fumbling improvisation. From the very moment of entry, the actions of the invaders followed a carefully detailed blueprint for a Communist state of Korea, to which Seoul was to be the key. It followed the pattern worked out during the five Communist years in North Korea, a pattern which, in turn, had found its model in Moscow and the European satellites. The speed and sureness with which the occupation forces operated in Seoul give good evidence of such careful planning. In the operation of the plan during Seoul's ninety days of Red occupation, we have the blueprint of the birth and development of a sovietized state. It provides one of the best glimpses behind the iron curtain that we have been permitted, and its understanding is of first importance to all peoples who still enjoy a free world.

The following pages describe this Communist blueprint at work in Seoul, partly as reconstructed by American social scientists who studied the city after its liberation, and partly as recorded by eminent Koreans who experienced the occupation.

In December 1950 the imminent return of the Reds forced the authors to make a hasty departure from Seoul. At the very last moment, they came upon a slight paperbound volume *This Is the Way I Survived,* a collection of the experiences of twelve Koreans during the three months of Red occupation. Soon afterward the Air Force discovered a second similar volume, *Ninety Days in Red Seoul.* Many of the contributors were persons who knew they must go underground because in their public lives their active opposition to Communism marked them for elimination. Others were persons who fled because they knew simply that they could not submit to Communist domination. They were primarily persons in the professions and government and while they are not representative of the Korean people as a whole, they are representative of thousands of people in the leadership group, the importance of which the Communists never underestimate.

Translated sections from both these collections of eyewitness accounts are scattered through the remaining pages as counterpoint to the analytical chapters. In most instances the narratives will illuminate some point or observation which has already been made. In others, however, the reader may be confused, for the testimony will appear contradictory. But this is part of the story of Seoul. It is in the nature of the case. In its details, it is neither lucid nor consistent; in its broadest outlines, it is all too horribly clear.

Chin-Ho Yu

The Reds Come to Seoul

Professor Yu, one of the framers of the R.O.K. constitution, had been marked by the Reds for liquidation.

About five o'clock in the afternoon of June 25 my second daughter (fifth year in Girls School) came home and said that the puppet army had crossed the 38th parallel. She said that in the city there were newspaper extras showing maps of the area with black arrows pointing out the directions the puppets were taking. It was so sudden I could not believe my ears. Hurriedly obtaining a paper, I found that what she said was true. At five o'clock that morning the puppets had started their invasion. Yet, even though the probability of invasion had given us much concern during the past years, what I read in the paper gave me no sense of reality or even of uneasiness. It was the faint booming of the cannons from the northeast that finally convinced me. I wondered if the sound came from Tongduchon or from Uijungbu.

Actually the puppet army had already captured Tongduchon and were now at the gate of Uijungbu. As my uneasiness increased I found it impossible to stay in the house. I went out to the highway in front of the College of Physics where I saw many jeeps and trucks rushing by, among them a big armored car, all laden with young soldiers, their faces keenly alert.

After supper I turned on the radio and listened, but there was nothing other than the regular program. I did not know whether the puppets had started a real war between north and south, or whether this was nothing more than a larger-scale quarrel over the 38th line. I had believed that a north-south war was possible as distinct from an American-Soviet Third World War, and yet I could not believe that the invasion today was the beginning of that war. In the National army occasionally some young officers talked of a northern expedition and bragged that the elimination of the 38th parallel would be no problem; but with some knowledge of our National army, I firmly believed that no such expedition would be made. Also, even though the reports had been conflicting, I could not believe that the puppet army was adequate in strength and equipment to attack us, or that the North would gamble on the indifference of the United States and the United Nations to attack the Republic of Korea.

Greatly troubled, I kept my seat by the radio, but except for Defense Minister Shin's short address at about midnight, there was no news or commentary of any kind.

At about two o'clock in the morning on June 26 I was half-aroused by voices in the street. I could not distinguish words, but I concluded that outside were people from Tongduchon who had been brought to Seoul by train, and I went to sleep again.

The next morning I should have gone to the Korean University to find out the state of affairs and to help decide upon the steps the school should take, but because of a lecture I was to give at the Public Officials' Training Center, I decided to go directly there. The jeep that was sent to take me to the Center from the suburb where we lived went out from the side street into the Chong-yangni Road. On the highway refugees were causing great confusion. There were men with loads on their heads and women with bundles on their backs. Some men were leading oxen, others were leading dogs, all looked very anxious.

While passing the Chong-yangni railroad station I could see no vehicles except streetcars—no buses, taxis, or any other kind of transportation. (The next day I found that they had been requisitioned by the army.)

Unlike Chong-yangni, in the city proper there seemed to be no refugees and things were quiet. The trainees at the Center were surprisingly calm. No one asked a question about the 38th parallel incident or showed any anxiety. But in order to quiet my own mind, I said, before beginning the lecture itself: "In serious times people often become excited, stop what they have been doing and talk and roam about the streets, but that is foolish. It would be better for those who study to keep studying in silence." Yet I myself could not concentrate on the lecture. Only the long habit of a classroom life enabled me to get through it. Later, I ran into Dean C. and he gave me the war news: Chunchon was already occupied and it seemed that the puppet army had arrived at Chongpyong Dam.

For the first time, I saw this war as a serious affair and different from former 38th parallel conflicts, an affair which might mean death for any of us, or for all of us. Yet the thought, "But how could it be?" persisted, and again I could not really feel that the war would reach Seoul.

Leaving the Training Center, I went to the Minjung

bookstore for my royalty check, and from there to Mi-jang Grill to keep an appointment with C. A farewell party was being given for Mr. R. who was to leave for the United States the next day to observe American newspaper work. Mr. Dong-Sung Kim and other acquaintances were there. From Mr. Kim I learned that Kaesong had fallen without resistance into the hands of the enemy. Many people in the city had been killed, and the fate of Mr. Kim's own family was unknown.

Many people came to the Grill, but those I was supposed to meet did not appear. I suspected that Mr. C., because of the work he was doing, would not come here for lunch when the situation was so serious, so I went out to the Chongno crossing. On the side of the Bell Tower were many posters reporting on the war. There was news about the Tongduchon and Uijungbu fronts, about the abandonment of Kaesong and the withdrawal to the Imchon River line. Somewhat encouraging was the report that an element of the National army had rushed into Haeju, but I wondered if it was not just an effort on the part of the Ongjin detachment to open a road to the main body when they found their road for retreat cut off at the sea.

At two o'clock that afternoon there was to be a meeting of the Central Educational Committee at the Department of Education. I telephoned the office, but neither the Minister nor the Vice Minister was there, and the secretary could only give uncertain answers to my questions. Since there was nothing I could do but waste time, I returned home.

About four o'clock I heard much noise of moving vehicles and when I went outside to look I saw National army contingents moving out to the front line. Here were the buses that were nowhere to be seen the day before, all loaded to capacity with young soldiers; some had the flag tied on their shoulders, others had it tied around their heads, and still others held it in their hands, while all sang a military song. As each vehicle passed, the people lining the street shouted "Mansei! [Hurray]" and clapped their hands. While watching, my eyes became moist and a comfortable feeling of "we live" came over me.

At about six o'clock that night, I telephoned the University President's residence to apologize for not having been to the college in the morning. We agreed that the situation was grave, but that there was nothing we could do immediately. We decided to meet the next morning at school. (Who could have guessed that this was to be our last conversation? Nothing has been heard from the President since he was taken north by the puppet soldiers.)

At six o'clock on the morning of June 27, when I was only half awake I heard the statement on the radio from the Office of Public Information that, "Because the enemy is nearing the capital, the Government is moving to Suwon." Unable to believe the news I had just heard, I kicked off the bedclothes, dressed, and went to the street to find there a rapidly increasing commotion. According to some passersby, the enemy had entered Chang-Dong; according to others, he had entered Jangui. No head nor tail could be made of the stories, but the sound of cannons told us that the enemy was very close.

I knew at that moment that I must escape. First of all,

I must have some money. I started to the Minjung bookstore to cash the check I had received the day before, but when I got to the end of the trolley line at Chongyangni, I felt I would not have time to do this, so I returned home. I found my brother-in-law there and I was thankful. I told my four little children to go to a relative's house under Inwang Mountain, and my wife and two bigger boys to stay home until there was danger the neighborhood would become a battlefield. I instructed my oldest daughter to go to R. immediately and ask if he would come and live in our house until the war was over. Then I put towels, paper and shirts in my briefcase, took some money from the house, and went out to the gate.

When my two youngest said goodbye I wanted to turn around and smooth their hair, but for fear I might shed foolish tears, I desisted. Even to my wife who came out to the gate I did not turn my head, but said simply, "There is no telling when we will meet again. Maybe after a few days; maybe after many years. Meanwhile we must survive; no matter what happens or what we do, we *must* survive." And finally, "I dare say they will not lay hands on my family." Then I left my family, my home, and my library. I had no sadness, no feeling. As if in obedience to some irresistible absolute order I left.

I went again to the end of the carline and looked around. For some reason, the cars that had been running a short while ago were no longer moving. I stood undecided. I heard the sound of big guns along with that of machine guns; it came from the north in the direction of Miari. As I looked around, I saw dense fog

—or smoke—under Neru Peak Mountain; it was too late, I thought. If Miari had become a battleground, I might be captured by the puppet soldiers before reaching the East Gate.

Yet I had no other choice than to try, so with my youngest brother-in-law who had joined me I began to walk toward the city. Nearing the East Station, I stopped a taxi almost forcibly, and unexpectedly a young man inside invited us to get in. There were already seven or eight persons in the taxi, and with the addition of the two of us the car was about to burst.

"Aren't you Professor Yu?" asked the young man. "I am a student at the College of Commerce. I studied constitutional law under you." I understood then why I was able to stop the car and was permitted to get in.

I wanted to go first to the Capitol Building, for before finally accepting my decision to take refuge, I had to know the true state of affairs. The taxi was going in the direction of South Gate and I got off at Chongno crossing. Just as I was turning the corner at the Whashin Department Store, Mr. S. came out of the crowd without a hat and with empty hands. When I told him I was on my way to the Capitol Building to get some news, he shook his head and said, "There's no one there." According to him, all those of ministerial rank seemed to have taken refuge and he, not knowing what to do, had remained with his subordinates up to a short while before when there had been an air raid. He was on his way now to make arrangements for his family.

Since there was no use in going to the Capitol, I decided to leave Seoul directly. While I was trying to think of how to get out, I remembered the Training Center jeep in which I had ridden yesterday. I decided to go to the Center and leave Seoul in that jeep.

I started walking toward Anguk-Dong. At the Center there were seven or eight government officials besides Mr. C. in the midst of some discussion. Their faces showed indignation rather than despair. It was maddening, after we had all talked so much about the puppets and the probability of attack, and had believed in our government and in our National Defense army, that in less than two days we had reached our present desperate situation.

"I should leave Seoul," I said, to get a reaction from them.

"Yes, Professor Yu should go, whichever way we look at it." They all urged me to leave immediately, but when I asked for a ride in their jeep they told me that it had been requisitioned the previous afternoon.

Coming out of the Training Center and standing at the crossing of Jae-Dong, everything before me looked black. At this rate I would not only be unable to leave Seoul, but would be captured by the puppet soldiers without ever having heard any authentic news of war. I could not decide what to do next. Perhaps if I went to the Police Bureau, I might find a jeep or a truck going south. But I was very tired and it was already past eleven. Yet I knew I couldn't dilly-dally any longer. I stood out in the middle of the street and, swallowing pride, held up my hand at every army or police car passing by. No one showed any willingness to stop. Everything was confusion. Most of the jeeps and trucks going east and west did not seem to be engaged in any organized public service. Everyone seemed to be in an insane hurry to save his own life. It was the animal instinct without propriety, shame, or self-respect. Suddenly I thought of my family, my home, and my books. I had left everything behind. I couldn't even get a ride in a car. Where am I trying to go, I asked myself. I felt anger and sadness all in the same moment. Of what use are the respect and standing due a scholar, writer, and professor? Here I was, a middle-aged man, divested of all dignity, wrestling with the question of life and death.

At this very second a ¾-ton truck stopped with a creaking sound right in front of me, and without more ado I got in. It was a police vehicle and there was an officer with the driver.

"Which way are you going?" asked the officer.

"Take me to the Seoul Police Bureau."

"This truck goes in the direction of Kyong Mu Dae," he answered.

Anger and despair gave me courage. I summoned my most military voice and said sternly, "Take me to the Seoul Police Bureau." He made no reply, but when the vehicle reached the front of the Capitol Building he ordered the driver to go on to the Police Bureau.

At the entrance to the Bureau I told the guard my name and walked in. But even greater disappointment awaited me for the Bureau was completely empty. Not even the Chief or the Vice Chief was there, but I heard voices coming from a small room where I found three or four plainclothesmen huddled together talking in undertones. It was good to have one of them greet me; he was K., a graduate of the Korean University. I asked whether there was a police vehicle going south from Seoul and was told there was none and that I had better inquire at the National Defense Department.

At the Bureau of Education and Information of the National Defense Department I found many army personnel busily at work. The Bureau Chief was out so I talked with Col. K., Chief of the Information Section. For the first time since the beginning of the war, three days ago, I got direct news from an authoritative person. Col. K. told me not to be pessimistic, since the American Air Force had begun action that morning. Yet, since the government had moved from Seoul, I wanted to leave too, and I asked Col. K. if there was a vehicle in which I might ride.

"There is no vehicle going down. However, you might wait a little and see," he replied. (This was the first and last time I ever saw the Colonel. I later read in the newspaper that he stayed at his post until the following day when he died a hero's death at the hand of puppet soldiers with burp guns.)

It was now nearly two o'clock and I was extremely distraught, but there was nothing else to do but wait. In a few minutes Mr. Dok-Kyen Choe came in with four or five other war reporters. When I told him that I was trying to leave Seoul he said, "Don't worry. We have come from the front and with our own eyes we saw American planes strike the enemy and put them to rout."

Although I found some comfort in this news, I still thought it better to leave Seoul. Even if the enemy tanks had retreated under the air attack, would they not come again after the planes had gone? And when they returned, how could our army, with no tanks, no planes, and no anti-tank guns, be able to defend Seoul against them. Since the enemy's mechanized unit, fronted by tanks, had entered Uijungbu, it was no time to stay in Seoul. Someone in the room remarked that the atmosphere in the streets was such that a riot might take place any time and I agreed. When Col. K. told me that a truck was going to the airfield and that I could go in it as far as Noryangjin, I thanked him warmly and followed the officer who was to go with the truck.

Camouflaged with leafy tree branches, with siren blowing, the military truck rushed along the South Gate Boulevard. The Boulevard was filled with a sea of people, but when we got to the Han River bridge not even the shadow of a man could be seen. Though I had no way of knowing it at the time, they were preparing to blow up the bridge then.

As we drove on toward Noryangjin I decided that when we arrived there, I would go to my sister's house and spend the night instead of continuing south. The American Air Force had after all struck and scattered the tanks; perhaps it would be possible to save Seoul.

As I alighted from the truck at Noryangjin and entered the alley to my sister's house, the quiet and peacefulness of the neighborhood made all the experiences of the last two or three days seem like a dream.

My brother-in-law met me in front of the house. I told him the urgency of the situation, but he did not seem to understand. Later, however, after we had gone into the house and talked for a while, I realized that he did know that danger threatened, but could not, himself, risk refuge because he did not even have money enough to buy food; he felt that he had to stay where he was so that he could sell clothing and furniture to buy something to eat. Since he had neither property nor name, it did not seem likely that the enemy would have any excuse to harm him or my sister. (This later proved to be a miscalculation. After the recapture of Seoul I returned and found that my sister had suffered from the puppets because she was related to me. She had to hide herself first in one place and then in another and barely escaped with her life.)

Somehow my arrival became known, and Y. and W. who lived in the same neighborhood came to ask if they could go south with me. But the radio continued to announce the coming of the American Air Force, and to say that the National army had been ordered to push on to the Yalu River. I kept hoping that Seoul would be saved, and wanted to wait a little while longer. Then I recalled what I had heard from Col. Kon-Suk Lee at the Aeronautic Officers School a month previously. According to him all the fighter planes of the puppets, excepting the Z model, were of 1,800 horsepower with heavy fire power, each costing about $100,000. The puppet army had in their possession at least a score of such planes and, together with the bombers, reconnaissance machines, and training planes, had altogether about 300 planes. Furthermore, such high-powered planes required pilots of many years' training, and the puppet army had been training pilots for about two years. Our army, on the other hand, had only about ten machines of 180 horsepower for training purposes and few pilots who could fly any of the new types.

The information about the puppets' planes had come

as a big surprise to the American Military Advisors who had maintained that there would be no need for planes in the event of a Korean war, and who did not, therefore, intend to give us any such aid.

With the National army without planes and pilots, would not the 200-odd planes of the puppet army use the southern sky at will as their proving ground? I at one time occupied an end seat in the government and have some knowledge of America's answer to our request for military aid. When I had heard Col. Lee tell of the puppets' planes, more than the might of the puppet army and the critical condition of our national defense, I had felt that the American attitude at that time was blameworthy. Fundamentally, what were the Americans thinking? Although the leftists are battling and pig-headed, compared with the rightist's feudal leaning and ideological poverty they are rightly or wrongly a unified aggressive force with a single objective. Without complete American support the democratic forces in this country might have disintegrated before they were drawn together; it was this support that had made possible the May 10 [1948] election and the formation of the Government of the Republic of Korea. Yet America's attitude after that is indeed hard for us to understand.

Even though it was announced that Soviet Russia was organizing a very large-scale army in the North and supplying an adequate quantity of arms, when the Americans withdrew, they left us with only a small carbine-equipped constabulary force. Not only that, but when we requested them to remain with us until our national defense was strengthened they, as if in compliance with the Communists' demand of "withdrawal of both armies," withdrew from this land without even a word of regret. Of course it is a fact that through the ECA America gave us an enormous amount of economic aid, but that aid was for economic reconstruction and not for armament. It is also a fact, however, that southern Korea could not produce planes and tanks in the economic rehabilitation program. Therefore, it is difficult for us to understand America's refusal to grant South Korea's urgent request for arms, especially modern arms. It could not be looked upon as anything other than the abandonment of Korea.

Toward evening my sister's daughter returned from the Girls' School near the East Station of Seoul. Somehow the streetcars that had not been running in the forenoon were back in service and she had ridden home without any difficulty. She unexpectedly brought me news of my family. "I met Wanni and Kyung-suk. As I was coming out of the school gate a cart passed, and Wanni and Kyung-suk were following it, singing and dancing." Wanni is my youngest boy and Kyung-suk is my youngest daughter. Following my instructions, they must have been on their way to the relative's house inside the city when my niece saw them. When she said they were singing and dancing behind the cart loaded with their things my chest almost burst.

Y. and W. came again to urge an early start for the south, but still I could not make up my mind to go. Later they came and again went away for still I had made no decision. I was as worried as they, but it was said that the war situation was getting better, and it was late in the day. Finally I decided to remain at my sister's for the night.

Things seemed to grow worse as time passed. The news on the radio was mingled with the sound of the cannons from outside. I listened with a burning heart and under the shower of cannon shells was oppressed by the thought that my family whom I had left might be dead. I was filled with remorse at having left them alone instead of risking all by bringing them out with me. But even if I had wanted to take the risk, where could I have taken six children to safety? If they were to die would it not be better for them to meet death at home than at the roadside? I had left them at home because it was said that the capital was being moved to Suwon, which meant unconditional abandonment of Seoul. If I had known that Seoul was going to be besieged I would not have left them there. But after the fact, no amount of thinking or regret can be of any help.

Suddenly I pricked up my ears. President Rhee, who had kept strangely silent since the breakout of the incident, was going to make a special broadcast. A few minutes later than the appointed time, the voice of the President was heard. He said that the friendly nations that had been aiding us had not trusted us quite enough to give us aid in arms in the past, but that such aid was going to come from now on; the speech concluded with a telegram from General MacArthur. The word that aid would come was reassuring, but to what extent and when would it come? The telegram gave no details.

Late that night I noticed that the rain had turned to drizzle. A few minutes later a strange sound came to my ears, like the sound of many people all speaking in guarded tones. I wakened my brother-in-law who slipped outside to return shortly with the information that people in the neighborhood were moving toward Sihenna and Kwachon. Did this mean that the enemy had already penetrated to this neighborhood? Would we be under gunfire here too? The fear of capture by the enemy even before dawn made me increasingly jittery.

After a while it was quiet again. I thought the refugees had all gone. Then piercing through the pattering of the rain drops was the sound of the engines of fast-moving motor cars. At first I did not think much about it, but when it continued for more than thirty minutes, I began to worry. I climbed up the stairs in darkness to the second floor and looked outside. On the highway in front of the Noryangjin station cars were running at full speed, with headlights that made a continuous stream of glittering lights.

All sorts of thoughts went through my head. The Government of the Republic of Korea! In those speeding cars must be the important persons of the political world—men in the army and police forces—military equipment, valuable articles and necessary documents. Then I was overcome by loneliness and hopelessness. I was moved to rush out and stop them, but that would not do, so I merely stood in silence and witnessed the scene. After about thirty minutes the noise and lights ceased and only the darkness surrounded me. Then I noticed that the sound of gunfire from the north was increasing its tempo.

With footsteps of hopelessness I turned back to my bedroom. My brother-in-law was sound asleep. I sat down before the glimmering candlelight. I wished to die—only to die. I would be in peace if death came now.

Suddenly there was an earth-shaking explosion and the house rocked. The Han River bridges are dynamited, I thought intuitively. There followed another explosion. My brother-in-law opened his eyes and got up. "The Han River bridges must have been blown up. Better go back to sleep," I told him. As for myself, I continued to sit and gaze at the candlelight.

I spent the rest of the night with my eyes wide open. The cannonade became more violent as the night wore on and toward dawn it came like thunderclaps, interspersed by machine-gun-fire. When it was daylight I went out to the yard. Smoke was coming up behind the hill in front of the house. It must have been from somewhere between the hill and Womsan, only the peak of which was visible. I knew that I had waited here too long. It had been five or six hours since the government went south, and now the enemy had come to Yongsan—the tank-led enemy was almost before me. Could my two legs go faster than the tanks?

A stream of refugees flowed to the south on the side-roads through Sihung and Kwachon. I stopped several of them and asked for news of the situation. Answers were all different. Some said the enemy had come to Samkachi, others said Yongsan had fallen, and still others that there was street fighting within the wall. Among the southward-bound refugees were some straggler soldiers and policemen in torn uniforms with lame legs and drooping shoulders. When I asked them news of the battle they merely continued on their way mumbling, "Couldn't fight without equipment."

My sister had breakfast ready, but I had no desire even to lift the spoon. When I came to think of it, I realized I had not had a morsel since the morning before.

Y. came again, all ready for the journey.

"Where do we go, if we go now?" I had no strength even to stand up.

"We should go as far as we can. Since the bridges are down, the enemy will not be able to cross so easily. Isn't that right?"

Instead of answering, I shut my eyes. It seemed that it would be better to stay here and get arrested than to start out now and later be captured on the road.

But a little later when W. came, somehow I was all on fire to leave. It seemed meaningless to stay and be arrested. So I gave some money to my sister to buy a few mals of rice and hurriedly left. But that frame of mind did not last very long either; as I climbed up the mountain pass behind the house my resolve changed again. What am I afraid of that I am running? What crime have I committed? Is death so terrible? Was I so attached to life, when death ends it all?

"I am not going," I said, and stayed my steps. W. was wide-eyed. I explained to him, "No matter how much I think about it, it's a face-losing affair. To be captured on the road while running away. . . ."

"So it would be." W. also stopped.

Returning to the house, I made a firm decision not to leave again. I buried the contents of my briefcase in the garden. I looked in the space above the ceiling thinking I would hide there if the enemy came. After this decision my mind was somewhat quieted, and I asked for the food I had refused a while ago—but still I could not eat it.

My anxieties refused to let me rest. In spite of my decision, about eleven o'clock I went out to the road again. The refugees had gone and only an occasional few were to be seen. A young man with a big cane came up to me. It was Mr. L. from the Educational Department. When we shook hands he asked me how I happened to be there and I explained. He seemed surprised, and told me that Teacher K. had left yesterday, taking his whole family with him. I felt hurt when I heard "the whole family." How is it that some people can move themselves and their families while one like myself has to go through all sorts of difficulties just to extricate myself from the danger area? I said aloud:

"How different he and I are. I left my family behind. . . . Why have I let seven die and saved my own life? I want to die."

"That's nonsense. Why do you talk that way?" Tears were dropping from L.'s eyes. "The American armed forces are coming, aren't they? If we hold out until then, the question is solved. I am going to Namhan Castle by way of Kwanak Mountain. In case we cannot keep the place, we will go to Chung-chang Province by way of Yaju and Ichon, following the mountain ranges." We said goodbye and L. walked on.

I did not move until L. disappeared over the hill, and then the thought "I must go" swept me off my feet. I hurriedly went back to the house and announced that I had really resolved to go. I dug up the things I had buried and put them in the bag. I burnt my visiting cards and identification card and left the house. My brother-in-law would go with me as far as Sihung where I might get a ride in a military vehicle, and if I made a good start there, he would let my family know of it. We went to Y.'s house, but it was empty. We also went to W.'s house, but he had already started.

I came to a point from which I could see Youngdunpo at a distance to the right. Scattered groups of refugees were plodding along. Some were already tired out and sitting by the roadside. Some asked me how the war situation was, trying to get news.

By the time I got to the Seoul-Pusan highway, I was one of those in the refugee line. There were many military vehicles coming and going and that gave me assurance that I would not be captured by the enemy on the road. So far it was a success. Just before Sihung station, a soldier came up in a jeep, megaphone in hand, announcing that the American army had landed. I could not rid myself of the thought that this was just an attempt to encourage the refugees.

"Where did they land?" I shouted at the soldier.

He looked hard at me and said, "My Uncle! what an improper question!" and drove on.

When I reached Sihung I felt that I was walking on the soil of the Republic of Korea again. At the gate of the officer's Artillery School the military police were inspecting all the on-coming vehicles and sending them in for reorganization.

Through the help of the military police I got a seat on a military vehicle going south, but it went only as far as Anyang and I had to get off there. I was now really in the midst of the refugees. Some families were pulling or pushing carts loaded with their meager belongings, worn and threadbare padded comforts, bags of rice, aluminum pans, etc. There were knapsack-carrying people, a farmer leading a cow, women carrying bundles on their heads. Never having had very much, one might think this part of the population would welcome the Communists, who would tell them they had been kept in the dark by the bourgeoisie and did not know what communism really is. But these people were fleeing, just as earlier millions under the Communist regime in the north had fled south at the very risk of their lives.

The refugees were divided into two streams, one following the main highway and the other the railroad track. I found myself, with two students who were headed for South Cholla Province, among the refugees following the railroad track. At Kumpo station I separated from the students, intending to return to the highway in order to enter Suwon by the North Gate. When I came out of the station I found myself on a different road and discovered that the highway was about two miles in the opposite direction. I went back into the station and looked east. Beyond a wide expanse of fields I saw the highway lined with rows of trees. To reach it I left the station precincts and walked north on a lonely road meandering between paddies and fields and used by oxcarts.

After walking a while I became tired and depressed! Where and in search of what am I going, after leaving the young loved ones, wife, books, desk, and all those things which I had been gathering like an ant for some fifty years? Then suddenly the picture of my youngest daughter and my last boy, who had been dancing and singing along behind the cart, appeared before me. To think that I had left them behind to the terrific gunfire was more than I could bear, and all my strength was sapped. I sat on a rock on the roadside and without my knowing it I crossed myself. I am an atheist and how I happened to use a religious sign, and why a cross among all the religious signs, I do not know.

When I was half across the plain, for the first time in two days I felt hungry. A hamlet was visible in a thicket on the sunny side. I dragged myself on lame legs to a yard where a woman was tending some barley straw and asked her if I could buy eggs. She looked up at me and said, "Come this way." I followed her silently and she came to a house with a gate of woven saplings. When she asked how many I wanted I told her two. She went in and after a while came out with two small eggs. I took them and handed her a 100-won bill, because in Seoul eggs cost 50 won each. She hesitated a little, then said she did not have the change and asked whether I would not take it in eggs. I assented, and she came out with two more. I ate three by making a hole at each end of the shell and sucking in the contents, and put the remaining one in my pocket. I offered my blessing upon the woman, the house, and the hamlet, and left with a lighter heart.

As I took the new main road among the refugees my mind was regaining confidence. I met a student who was on his way to his wife's relatives in Kongju, and I also met the former National Assemblyman C. A jeep whisked by, and in it I glimpsed the face of Dr. H. of the American Embassy, and also Professor B., our former envoy to the Philippines. I was about to hail them, but on second thought I decided that since I had walked this far I could walk the remaining seven miles.

The seven miles were so long it was tantalizing. Always before, the avenue on the west, flanked by old pine trees with hanging branches had seemed only a short step from the North Gate of Suwon. But then I had been in a car and now, although from under the pine trees I could see the Gate right there, the more I walked the farther away it seemed to get. I rested every ten minutes, and every time I got up it was more painful than ever, but I could not help resting. Every time I passed a house I went in and asked for water and drank in big gulps.

While resting at the North Gate, I stopped some people and asked where the Government was, but no one knew. I suddenly recalled that during the election I had met a Mr. R. who was in the newspaper business here, and I thought that if I could find him I would get some news and learn the whereabouts of the Government.

At the Chongno [Bell Street] crossing I saw a small sign pointing to the operations section of the MacArthur forces. My eyes brightened. What I had heard from the soldier in a jeep at Sihung must be true! Democracy had worked a miracle!

Generally, the shortcoming of democracy is its slowness to act. Communism to the contrary is non-controversial and quick in action. The Communists know this weakness of democracy, and that is why they started this war. Whether the United Nations passed a resolution against them or not, if they could blitz down to Pusan and Mokpo before either the United Nations or the United States could take effective action, victory would be theirs. In the past, organizations for the maintenance of international peace had been lacking in real strength. But now, right there before me was the signboard which announced the operations section of the MacArthur forces. It was a miracle: no more than three days after the start of the conflict in Korea over fifty nations were rising up to punish the aggressor.

In the neighborhood of the newspaper office swarmed all kinds of people. Here and there were many familiar faces. For the first time since the start of the invasion, the army, police and people were in high spirits. The reorganized army elements passed in a stream to the north, singing the army songs.

"Tonight the Daredevil Police Brigade will enter Seoul. Within tomorrow we will recapture the city," whispered K. into my ear. A delay would mean more sacrifices of life, so the police were going to cross the Han River that night and storm their way in. . . .

Who could have known that Seoul would be left to the iron heels of the enemy for ninety days?

The Blueprint of Occupation

Perhaps the most striking feature of the Communist preparations for taking over South Korea was the meticulous care with which they were made. The political leaders, of course, had been predetermined with considerable care and were organized to take over their new functions at a moment's notice. Tons of leaflets, posters, and propaganda materials had been printed, stored in freight cars, and held at the 38th parallel awaiting word of the occupation of Seoul. Files of complete dossiers on key South Korean personnel were brought into Seoul almost simultaneously with the military forces. Lesser administrative personnel, especially police officials, had been appointed for various positions in South Korea and stood in readiness at the 38th parallel. A considerable training program, extending over at least a three-year period, had been conducted in Pyongyang for highly selected South Korean personnel. Plans were on hand for rapid introduction of the North Korean system of land reform; local Communist Party secretaries were already appointed, and puppet mayors had been spotted for the key cities and villages. A modified North Korean legal system was ready for operation; and elaborate preparations in the fields of taxation, labor legislation, and methods of "electing" the various People's Committees were already in hand.

Despite the detail of these preparations, it was apparently the intention of the occupying authorities to give the impression that most of this work had actually been accomplished in Seoul during the first days and weeks of occupation. The illusion that local people were to be selected for key positions in the new regime was carefully fabricated. The theory obviously was that an appearance of efficiency and practicality *at the local level* would convince the people of Seoul of a widespread acceptance of the occupying forces.

In one respect, however, this theory backfired. The tangible evidence of the hated dossiers which were bursting from the briefcases of North Koreans when they entered Seoul furnished conclusive evidence of long and detailed planning. The testimony of a mother of three children whose husband, an ex-official, entered the R.O.K. army after hiding out in Seoul for three months, is typical: "They made in advance a list of those reactionaries they wanted to arrest. The police system was well prepared, and the North Koreans trained in the general methods of the Soviet system. . . ." Others reported that: "They were well organized and prepared. For instance, every supervisor of all the organizations was appointed beforehand. . . ." "Everything they planned to do was put into action quickly . . . their things were very systematic."

What kind of program, then, warranted such careful preparation? A system of "thought control" and the imposition of a new political hierarchy—these were the two dominant elements in the Communist blueprint.

Thought Control

In many ways the program to control thought was the most pervasive part of Communist activity. Some form of propaganda was associated with literally everything that the invaders did. Their soldiers were taught to pay Korean women the uncommon tribute of a handshake as a symbol of the equality of the sexes. When the People's Committees announced redistribution of the land, they seized the opportunity to include in the announcement a little lecture on the nature of the People's Republic and the workers' state. When the police collected sewing machines from the people of Seoul, ostensibly for use in hospitals, they berated the U.N. forces for their brutality and emphasized how gloriously, in contrast, the People's Republic cares for its wounded and unfortunate. When their officials began the difficult and potentially unpopular task of remaking the schools, they appointed a front committee to demonstrate the popular nature of the new movement. There was no occasion too insignificant to omit the chance of trying to pound into the people the idea that it was their great good fortune to be living in a Communist state.

Since ideas in any totalitarian state are an aspect of power, the control of information is considered of equal importance to other controls. The strenuous efforts to attain a Communist monopoly on communication in Seoul—suppression of newspapers, nationalization of all mass communications, control of content, exclusion of non-Communist news services and printed material, confiscation of radios to keep out the U.N. broadcasts even at the sacrifice of the Communists' own broadcasts—represent measures for thought control which startle the free world. They are an integral part of the Communist state, however, and follow the same pattern as control of political and economic activity.

Three principles—monopoly, reinforcement, and concentration—seem to have governed the program of thought control in Seoul during the summer of 1950. Eliminate every non-Communist source of information possible. Repeat and repeat a message through every possible channel. Concentrate on a relatively simple line and carefully and logically relate new material (for instance, news and new programs) to it. They were "shotgun" communicators. Repetition did not worry them. They wanted to be as sure as possible that no target was missed, that any given message would be dinned unforgettably into every ear through every channel.

Propaganda itself was simple, intense, bitter. It vilified the U.S. and R.O.K. governments. It sang hymns of praise and affection for the U.S.S.R. and the North Korean government of Kim Il Sung. It also made promises intended to be attractive to broad groups among the South Koreans. The North Korean Reds promised a united and free Korea, land distribution and nationalization of industry, equal status for women, a broad program of social betterment, lower prices and an assured living for workers, and more efficient and honest government.

They would unite Korea by sweeping away the artificial barriers, and the whole nation would work together toward a glorious tomorrow. They would free Korea from imperialists "like the United States," and "corrupt and inefficient representatives" like those now in the Rhee government; the common people of Korea would determine their own destiny. The land, they said, must be owned by those who farm it. Therefore, it would be confiscated from the large owners and redistributed equally and without charge to the farmers. The profits of industry like the ownership of land would be redistributed to the workers. "Women," they claimed, "are no longer slaves." They pointed out that licensed prostitution and concubinage were practically at an end in North Korea, and that jobs and appointments were open on an equal basis to both men and women. So it would be, they promised, in South Korea also. They predicted employment for all, with an eight-hour day, annual vacations (twenty days' recreation at a health resort every year), a medical program and public hospitals, better care for old persons and orphans, social insurance, more schools, and easier access to them for the children of the proletariat. By the end of July the war would be won, and early in August the government would be moved from Pyongyang to Seoul; general elections would be held by August 15, 1950.

For nearly everyone in South Korea, these promises held both a general and a specific interest. On the people of Seoul, land distribution, equal status for women, and a united Korea seemed to have made the greatest impression. There is little doubt that many of these people approved the program presented; as a result, the occupation period began with a great deal more cooperation and acceptance than would otherwise have been possible.

The occupation government not only made promises, it also outlined what must be done to make them come true. To solve the social problems, to achieve freedom and strength for Korea, it would be necessary to "destroy, then build"—to get rid of the traitorous leaders, the unfriendly foreign influences and the outworn institutions, and build anew by means of hard work and proper organization. It was conveniently necessary, therefore, to express itself specifically and at length on the governments involved in the proposed changes—the United States, the Republic of Korea, and the U.S.S.R.

The United States was pictured as the prototype of the imperialistic, colonial past. "Imperialist" was the word always associated with the United States in Communist propaganda, and the one name that stuck. The United States wants to make Korea its colony, the Communists said, and the Rhee government is for all practical purposes "a colonial government." The chief interest of the United States in Korea is to provide "a market for its products, which are already flooding Korea." The United States isn't working out of benevolence for the Korean people, but rather "to exploit and enslave them." Much was made of the fact that the United States provided sugar with which the R.O.K. government established a candy factory. "What kind of help for Korea are candy factories?" the Communists sneered. The United States, they said, is the leading reactionary country in the world. It represents class and property distinction and race discrimination. Finally, the United States has been responsible for this war by forcing the South Koreans to invade North Korea. On this point a little later the line changed slightly to: "The United States is responsible for prolonging the war by intervening in a Korean civil conflict."

The United States was always referred to with bitterness and hatred, but the choicest epithets were reserved for the R.O.K. government of Syngman Rhee, "the running dog of American imperialism," the "puppet of American imperialism run by warmongers of Wall Street." His was a "putrefied" "corrupt" government. He and his followers were "traitors," "murderers of 250,000 patriotic Koreans," and "exploiters of the poor South Korean people for their own private interest." Their basic argument was that the Rhee government, insofar as it was not more than a U.S. puppet, was corrupt and inefficient. It was always compared unfavorably with the North Korean government. The Republic of Korea was "government of a privileged class," whereas there was no division of classes in North Korea, a "paradise for diligent people." The South Korean government was "an old tree in autumn whose leaves are falling," whereas the North Korean government was "a young tree in spring which would bear green leaves and fruit." In South Korea the people were hungry and the industries were lying idle, but North Korea had plenty of work and food for everyone. Without American aid, the Rhee government did nothing, but the North Koreans made their own world. Reasons like these, therefore, had made it necessary for the People's army to come down from North Korea and save the people "groaning under the South Korean government."

Even the praise for Kim Il Sung and his diligent North Koreans, however, could not equal the orchids reserved for Stalin and Russia. The superlatives among their graded adjectives were always saved for Stalin and his government. For a time an effort was even made to refer to Russia as "the fatherland," but there are indications that this was not well received and had to be abandoned. But Russia remained "the great emancipator," "emancipator of weak races," "wall of democracy," "liberator of the working class," and, of course, "Korea's greatest friend." It was entirely with the help of the Soviet army that Korea was emancipated, the Seoul people were told. The Russians fought the Japanese in North Korea but the Americans did not shed a drop of blood for Korea. Russia has helped Korea with materials, technical aid, and spiritual guidance—all without any selfish motive (in contrast to the imperialistic, greedy United States). Although Russia was a peaceful country, should war come, it would prove itself to be also a very powerful country, one that would win in a short time. Thus, Russia was presented as Korea's special friend, and the world-wide leader of weak races and oppressed and peaceloving people against imperialists, exploiters, and aggressors.

Frequent attempts were made to connect the R.O.K. government and the United States with the Japanese who were so generally hated in Korea. R.O.K. leaders were accused of shipping grain to Japan even though some of their own countrymen were hungry. The United States was repeatedly charged (after June 28) with using Japanese troops in its Korean forces.

The propaganda line directed at the South Koreans was remarkably consistent with the line that had been used previously in North Korea; it was also closely akin to all the other Communist lines in Asia, a fact which pointed to central correlation if not central control. It was laid on with the usual Communist saturation technique. Unfortunately, it can be safely said that the South Koreans learned the main lessons and made the main associations that the Communists intended, because even four months after the occupation, the citizens of Seoul still repeated freely the idea clusters and the favorite adjectives.

The Political Hierarchy

Of primary importance in the Communist blueprint was the establishment of new lines of authority that would control individually and collectively every man, woman, and child in Seoul.

The basic design for such a system had already been worked out in the organization of the Party itself and had been tried out in other places including North Korea. Men, women, and children were considered as three separate responsibilities. Party members were directly responsible for the adult male population, and the Women's Alliance and Youth Alliance took care of women and children, respectively.

As in the organization of the Party itself, at the top of each of these three hierarchies was a small cadre of highly trusted Party members whose identities were unknown to the lower echelons, and from whom all orders came. Organized under these top men were three People's Committees: the city, sectional and village committees. The city People's Committee served as the real operational arm and disseminated specific instructions and plans. The sectional People's Committee was subdivided into as many subsections as were necessary. In Seoul there were five main sections, and each section was further subdivided into units sometimes as small as to concern no more than ten to a dozen homes. The village People's Committee varied in size and usually operated under instructions from one of the sectional committees.

The operation of all these committees was further controlled by an organized secret check on all their activities. The top men constantly checked on the activities of the city committee, and a highly secret overseeing committee checked on the operations of the sectional and village committees, who knew of its existence but never knew who its members were.

Perhaps no single characteristic of the Communist power system is as pervasive as this principle of hidden authority in back of all formal authority. All nominal executive heads in Seoul, for example, had considerable responsibility, but on all important decisions they were constantly referred "to the North." In most instances, there was also some aura of mystery surrounding the source of orders as, for example, the orders that came every day to the Youth Alliance. In such an organization, one knew only the man from whom one received the order and the man to whom, in turn, the order was given; the original source was hidden. And, as if to make doubly sure, the secret police were everywhere. They operated throughout the ministries, offices, and factories without their identities being known even to the Communist-appointed executives in those organizations.

Interestingly enough, however, the fact of the secret nature of this whole operation gradually became a matter of common knowledge in enlightened circles. This was certainly true of many non-Communists who managed to stay on in lesser clerical positions in the various ministries. The statement of a technician in the Ministry of Commerce and Industry is typical: "I knew that there was somebody pulling the wires behind the chairman of the city committee, and that even the extreme left-wingers themselves were being watched."

For the population as a whole, of course, it is much more difficult to judge the extent of this awareness, yet the available evidence indicates that the great majority of the educated population who remained in Seoul during the occupation was fully aware of what was going on. A teacher in one of the high schools expressed a common point of view when he said: "Neither the Red mayor, Li-Sung Yup, nor the chairman of the Seoul City Communist Committee were the 'big shots.' The 'big shots' were in Pyongyang. Perhaps, the Supreme People's Committee of the People's Republic of Korea was the powerful executive organ."

Yet, at the same time, there was also a persistent feeling among some of the better educated residents of Seoul that the seat of authority was to be found neither in Pyongyang nor "to the North," but in Moscow. A newspaper man reported that: "All the instructions [for Seoul] came from Pyongyang, and these in turn came from Soviet Russia. Even the vice-premier, Myung-Hee Hong, was regarded as non-Communist by real Communists. That shows that even some of the cabinet members of North Korea had no decisive words to say." An assistant museum curator said it more simply: "The authorities lived in Pyongyang, getting their instructions from Moscow."

One of the best illustrations of the planned sovietization of South Korea may be seen in the formal organization of the Home Ministry. Geared to guarantee all aspects of internal security, it ran the gamut from the "thought police" to border intelligence, from the statistical analysis of population movements to the clothing requirements of company-level cultural officers.

Although the critical question as to the precise relationship which existed between the Home Ministry and the Party cannot at the moment be answered, it is nevertheless clear that the key positions in the Ministry were held by highly trusted Party members. Furthermore, the fact that the Ministry was organized along military lines perhaps indicates better than any one single fact the essential nature of the Soviet master plan. An organizational chart captured in Pyongyang by advance R.O.K. troops, with notations applicable to Seoul, supplies further details. For example, all the police reported to the Home Minister, so did the fire fighters, the railway guards, and the several units of border guards. Equally interesting is the extent of the organization for equipment and supplies and the various provisions for indoctrination and education—the staff school, the cultural (indoctrination) bureau, the office in charge of the re-education of political prisoners. The complete plan was brought to Seoul and used as the model for the Ministry of Home Affairs set up in late June, 1950. It was apparently intended, after a quick victory and the projected national elections in South Korea, to consolidate the central control functions in North and South Korea into one national Korean organization.

Some of the best illustrations, however, of the careful

planning of the Communist organization for the control of power are to be found not in the large overall blueprints, but in the "logical" extension of master plans to the points of their contact with the people.

One very specific evidence, in fact, of the inseparable relationship between the political hierarchy and the communications monopoly is to be found in the various ways in which the power organizations were used for the purposes of indoctrination and propaganda. The organizational chart of the Home Ministry lists a complete cultural bureau and a separate cultural unit for the guard bureau; a staff school for the indoctrination of the entire personnel and a special office for the re-education of political prisoners. This entire group of "cultural" agencies within this one organization is quite separate and distinct from the Ministry of Information, the agency specifically concerned with matters of propaganda and culture. Every agency, every official organization, every unit of the army had its own cultural machinery.

The organization of the district headquarters of a gun (district) Youth Alliance is a good example. Those members of the organization who were not chiefs or assistants were assigned to duties in the various sections. The education section was in charge of the Youth Alliance program in the schools; the cultural section, in charge of the preparation of materials and programs for indoctrination; the registration section, in charge of keeping tab on young people and prospective young Communists; and so on. The leaders were in charge of meetings. Country and city headquarters reported to one of these district headquarters. All were organized in the same general pattern, all—according to the available testimony—were "busy as bees."

That such meticulous division of labor in the new "tradition" for South Korea was no accident may be seen through a brief glimpse into one aspect of the North Korean army. For here is a miniature version of the Soviet master plan. Here is the formula for Seoul—a careful blending of thought control and formal authority.

In the North Korean 7th divisional headquarters, for example, the propaganda section was as highly organized as any other section in the division. Headquarters consisted of a commanding general, an assistant commanding general, and four senior colonels, each of whom headed a section. Culture officers, reporting to divisional headquarters, were spaced through all units down to the company. Testimony from North Korean prisoners of war indicates the great influence of these officers. One captured officer claimed that the propaganda officer was the most powerful section head in the division. The importance of the indoctrination of North Korean soldiers by these culture officers is evident from an abundance of testimony. One prisoner of war testified that he was inducted on August 15, 1950, was given Communist indoctrination from August 16 through August 18, spent three days in travel, and then after four days' military training went into battle. With only seven days for any kind of training, it was considered necessary to spend nearly half the time in indoctrination!

It cannot be emphasized too strongly that this careful organization for indoctrination purposes, linked as it was to the structure of formal authority, was not restricted to the army or to the preparation of soldiers, it was also a part of all civilian preparation for life in a Communist state. For instance, to take one example out of many, all medical students in North Korea were obliged to have their programs arranged to include one and one-half hours of Communistic indoctrination daily. Anyone who missed these classes or was heard to make "reactionary" comments was severely punished. When the medical student graduated and moved into a professional association which also, of course, was tightly organized into a political hierarchy, he continued to have a "cultural" hour for indoctrination purposes every afternoon. And even the patients who received treatment for their physical ills in the hospital at Pyongyang received at the same time political indoctrination from cultural officials.

Clearly, then, the control system of the Communists was no empty gesture. It was cleverly and specifically designed to reach all segments of the population, and to insinuate itself into all aspects of Korean life.

Kun-Ho Lee

The Character of the Invader

Kun-Ho Lee is the author of several widely known volumes on Korean law.

In trying to write about the ninety days of ordeal, I find the memory of the daily threat to life too fresh to know what to tell and how to tell it. All of us who remained in the area had similar experiences and feelings; what we say may seem to the reader commonplace and even shallow. But be that as it may, the object of the writer is to supply materials for reflection.

"Tomorrow morning General MacArthur, the Supreme Commander of the Allied Powers, will establish headquarters in Seoul, and the superior U.S. air forces will cut off the advance of the Communist army. The people of the city are urged to ease their minds," blared the radio. Simultaneously the refugees from Chongyangni and Miari poured into Seoul and the sound of gunfire came nearer. The streets of Seoul looked desolate, not because they were empty but because everyone seemed so disconsolate.

That evening Mr. R., the leader of the neighborhood class [ten households form one class], came to consult with me. I told him that basing my judgment on what we had heard from those who came south after August 15, 1945, about the barbarity of the Soviet soldiery, and on what I had read in two or three books concerning the cruelties and violence of the Communists, it would be best to take refuge in case Seoul fell. Mr. R.'s view coincided with mine, because he had heard from refugees that the Communist soldiers shoot people without discrimination and perpetrate massacres and wanton destruction. We decided to leave together and separated to pack our necessary belongings.

Now as the sound of gunfire came closer, refugees from Tonam-Dong and Songbuk-Dong were pushing in, in addition to those from Miari and Chong-yangni. Not only did we hear the sound of cannon fire we also heard machine gun fire quite distinctly. My wife, faced with the solemn reality of a situation that she had never even imagined, did not know what to do and was simply weeping. The rain was drizzling, and to keep the little ones from catching cold, their underwear, stockings and changes of clothes were put in two knapsacks. In the turmoil we missed our supper. We took our four children—eight altogether in the party—and stood out in the vestibule. My wife, crying, said that she had never dreamed of acting out what she read in *I Crossed the Thirty-eighth Parallel* [title of a book written by a Japanese authoress, giving her experiences from Chang-Choon to the 38th after the Japanese surrender]. Our seven-year-old boy, the eldest, who is always jubilant when we go anywhere, danced about with joy.

The sound of rifle fire told us that the enemy had already set foot in Seoul. Mr. R. could not be seen anywhere and the members of the neighborhood class as a whole decided to remain, seeking shelter from bullets in the basement, under the floor, etc. Where could we go with a man of seventy and four young ones at this trying moment? Finally, we decided against escape and re-entered the house.

I had never before heard the gunfire of a real battle;

it sounded like a cruel signal for the ending of life. Strangely enough at this moment, I found I had an irresistible desire for coffee, and I drank three strong cups. Then I sent the whole family into a low closet and, sitting before the fireplace in the kitchen, I began to think about the past thirty-four years. A sadness came over me as I sat there and I felt a new sense of emptiness. Wishing to see the faces of the little ones, I crept into the closet. There was no lamp, but the innocent faces were visible in an indistinct way, and sorrows overflowed the bosom that had nothing to lean against.

Something heavy fell in the next house, probably a stray shell. Purposely I avoided looking at the clock and did not try to find out what made the noise. Then someone screamed, but I would not admit to myself that it was a human cry. The blind hope remained that if the day broke very quickly General MacArthur's headquarters would come to Seoul and save us. My wife seemed to be constantly worried as to the time.

Then someone knocked hard at the door of the vestibule and called out, "Professor Lee, Professor Lee." I went to the door and found K., a friend from Tonam-Dong, with his wife and two children. When they came in K. said, "It seems certain that the Communist army is going to occupy Seoul. Already they have come to Tonam-Dong. The Communists are said to massacre South Koreans as reactionaries without discrimination. What are we to do? If we survive the fighting, we will be murdered as reactionaries." K.'s intrusion made the household all the more uneasy and nervous. Our conversation ended in an Oriental fatalism: let come what may; if not death, it will be life.

After making room for them, we covered ourselves with many folds of blankets, as a partial protection against shrapnel, and listened. It was certain that the gunfire was only a few hundred yards away for the house shook and the windows rattled.

The night of the 27th dawned at long last into the 28th, and the ninety-day ordeal began. About seven o'clock there was much noise outside. The Communist army was reported to have entered the city with several hundred, maybe several thousand, vehicles in the lead. Soon after the army's entrance, the walls were plastered with posters of "People's Army, Mansei!" and a stern order for the display of the Communist flag was issued. Later, taxis, trucks, and jeeps on the streets flew the flags, and posters on the walls bore slogans of "Kim Il Sung, Mansei." Pictures of Kim Il Sung and Stalin were at all the important places.

Placards and signboards in the name of "Committees," "Alliances" and "Associations" were in great abundance. "The American imperialism would have made you, our compatriots, migrate to South America. We have saved you before it happened." When one South Korean read it, he turned around with a smile and said, "Our worry is that we *cannot* go to South America. Rather than to live under you it would be far better to live even in the South Pole." Another poster said that America sent us spoilt flour and candy, but a passerby who read this one said, "They haven't even let us see a grain of millet." But the people's reaction did not seem to bother the puppets.

The so-called People's army was composed of surprisingly young boys. There was a group of young girls also. Each of them had a "dabal gun" [the so-called "burp" or sub-machine gun]. It was surmised that some of them were Soviet soldiers, but I did not see any, although it seemed quite certain that there were Chinese Communists among them. The soldiers began to swagger around, ordering this and that in their terrible Hamkyang provincial accent.

First of all, they started vigorously to "liquidate the reactionaries." The terrible "liquidation," I hate to remember it even. They announced the opening of the so-called "People's Court." In effect this organization massacred innocent people. My older aunt who was an eyewitness related this:

> When a strict order came for all the inhabitants of East Soong-Dong to gather at the athletic ground of the College of Physics, I went without an inkling of what was to happen. The Communists with rifles and burp guns brought in a number of bound young men, and said, "Now we are going to begin the People's Court." Then a fellow among them who wore an armband said in a loud voice that the one who was under arrest was an evil person and he was to be shot for so and so reasons. Then he asked if anyone was opposed to it. Who would dare say anything in opposition, even though all the people gathered there felt it was not right and pitied the victim? Opposition meant losing one's own life. The onlookers were as silent as a dead mouse. Then the fellow with the armband said, "I recognize that you all favor it. The execution will take place right here." So saying he made the victim sit down with his back turned and they shot him.

No one would tell when and upon whom this sort of devilish judiciary farce would be enacted. If anyone incurred the displeasure of these comrades with the armbands, a summary trial resulted and there could be no "opposition." These were omniscient and omnipotent prosecutors, judges and executors put together. And since during three years of U.S. military government and two years of R.O.K. government there was hardly a person who had not done something to arouse the ire of these Neros, those who managed to escape the stray bullets were nearing the day of death as reactionaries.

My brother-in-law, the Education Promotional Worker of the Metropolitan Provincial Government, came to discuss the question of taking refuge. He was worried because of the fact that he had expelled a good many Red teachers. I myself had given lectures on anti-Communism and had written anti-Communism and anti-Soviet articles for several newspapers and magazines. K., the poet, who had done radio broadcasts about North Korea, had disappeared after he was said to have been arrested by the secret police. Anyway, it did not appear possible to stay at home safely. I thought up a plan: early each morning I would leave home and spend the whole day in my uncle's house listening to the radio, returning home just before curfew. If, as I suspected, the Political Security Bureau or the Internal Affairs Office [Police], or the People's Court paid me a call, they would not find me at home.

About July 10th the invaders began to make an abrupt change in their policy. Up to that time they said that they would not oppress the liberals, would allow private property, and that the people should go on with their business with their minds at ease. They had tried to buy the good will of the people and gain free assistance, but now they began to apply pressure without compunction.

There appeared to be a number of reasons for this change. First, influenced by America, the U.N.'s reaction was surprisingly strong. They did not keep their hands off the Korean question, and so the defeat and destruction of the Communist army was "as clear as looking at a fire." The puppets, therefore, tried every method to strengthen their position.

Second, contrary to what the North expected, the people of the South were found to be so "reactionary" that they not only showed unwillingness to cooperate but they also engaged in hostile activity. It may be also that they hoped first to soften the property class and liberals and then strike them quickly. The so-called voluntary surrender method is an example. It was announced that whoever surrendered would be given clemency, but many of those who did surrender were either imprisoned or met unknown fates. A relative of the wife of a police officer surrendered and died in prison. My fellow alumnus K., because he was formerly a prosecutor, surrendered and has never been heard of again. Voluntary surrender was a clever trick by which they could arrest people without effort.

The war situation may also have influenced the Communists to change their tactics. Korea was the first military action since the establishment of the United Nations, and the United Nations would probably call up all its resources to make this the most powerful and effective international intervention ever undertaken. Though the National army and the U.N. forces seemed to be on the run, they were yet full of confidence, and the Communist army that appeared to be winning was full of anxieties. "When all the manpower and material resources are mobilized and expended, then what?" Questions like this from the "Voice of America" must have chilled the breast of the Communist army. However they reasoned, the fact remains that they soon put aside their hypocritical mask and resorted to brutal and repressive measures.

Although the Communists' policy changed in detail from time to time, basically it was nothing but bestiality. The omnipresent appeal of Kim Il Sung was to "liquidate the reactionaries, non-cooperators and escapees without mercy." But citizens remained unwilling to cooperate and did everything possible to escape. When the American air force began its raids, the patriotic underground civilians threw signal bombs on Communist installations in an effort to direct the raid. Mimeographed newspapers containing news made public by the Office of Public Information of the Republic of Korea were circulated. From the pictures of Kim Il Sung and Stalin posted on the walls somebody always took the eyes out. As these things went on, repression by the Communists grew worse and worse; but as the repression grew worse, the resistance of the civilians became stiffer. Had the North Koreans been subjugating a completely foreign nation, the repression could not have been worse; they treated us completely as slaves.

Whispering started among civilians, and at times there were open conflicts: "The Red army shall be destroyed! The National army and the U.N. forces will soon enter the city. Then what is the thing for us to do? The intelligent civilians know. No matter how violently you treat us or how miserable you make it for us, is not the final outcome very clear? You brag about being for the people, but what is it that you do? You have not even let us see a quart of barley or a pint of flour and have not cared whether the people starve or not; and what sort of friends of the people are you? You are bandits feeding only yourselves. What sort of liberators and heroic fighters for the democratic revolution are you? It's all lies. We are sick of it." These outcries of the people came from the depth of their hearts. There was no reason to cooperate, for the people saw the Red bandits for what they were.

The Communists' growing repression and oppression included the so-called "migration," the "Volunteer Corps," and the "mobilization of labor."

It was toward the end of July that "migration" was first spoken of. At first no one knew enough about it to be either for or against. Actually, it meant that the population was to be decreased by one-half. Each section of the city had a given allotment of migrants who were to be forced out, for "too great a density of population made it difficult to take protective measures against air raids." But was it so? Their propaganda statements were rich in beautiful promises. "You, the beloved populace of the city! In the northern half of the People's Republic, democratic work during the last five years has progressed with achievements. If you migrate to the northern half, there is waiting for you ample food, housing, furnishings, and places of occupation. Take only those things you need in your travel on the road and start for the North." What transparent lies they were. What "democratic work" was so productive of "achievements" that everything was in readiness for the migrants from Southern Korea? A neighbor who under pressure had gone beyond the 38th parallel, came back and said, "Following their direction a group of us went beyond the 38th line but were told that nothing was ready for us. There was nothing for us to do but to return to Seoul. When I came back to my house I found a stranger living there, and the clothing and chests they had promised to take care of for us were nowhere to be found."

The Communists would order a house to be vacated by a certain date. "In the People's Republic rules are strict," they threaten. "If the house is not turned over, it will be very unpleasant." "Unpleasant" may or may not mean the burp gun, but this emigration order created a whirlwind of fear in the city. After being wrested of home and belongings, where can one go? The object of migration seemed to be, first, a revenge for non-cooperation; second, to make the majority of the city population propertyless so that they would have to cooperate; third, dispersion of the so-called reactionaries; fourth, the Communists wanted the houses and belongings; and fifth, to facilitate street fighting in case the National army entered the city.

The question of the Volunteer Corps came up about July 15th. At first there was a pretense of recruiting volunteers, and there was no evidence of impressment. The Communists even fixed the qualifications for volunteers so that only the Labor Party members, ex-prisoners, and the extremists could apply. But as the tide of war turned against them and they could not keep the facts from the people, they began to use pressure. Posters were placed on all street corners at random. "With our own hands let us crush the 'enemy'; join the Volunteer Corps!" "Those 'rascals' are not more than a handful, we must join the Volunteer Corps and capture them with our own hands and kill them!" In this vein they carried on their propaganda, but the people were not fooled; recruiting was a complete failure. They substituted arrest. They arrested young men and put them in the corps and used them as cannon fodder. The name "young men" was a misnomer, because I happen to know a man fifty-four years of age who was taken in. "His Excellency" Kim Il Sung (they never fail to use that title for Kim) issued a mobilization order taking in all men up to thirty-seven years of age, and it was recorded in newspapers, but there was no reason whatsoever for us to obey such an order.

At key points in the city, groups of extremists—the members of Communist young men's and young women's organizations—were stationed to catch people for their army. People used all kinds of methods to elude them, and many succeeded.

The Communists devised another method of forcing the people into their army. A distant relative of mine, who was employed at the Electric Company, on a certain day heard the siren blow calling everyone to the hall. When he got there a fellow went up on the platform and announced that a "Down with American Imperialism" mass meeting had been called. Then he pounded the table, made a rapid speech, and proposed that all present join the Volunteer Corps. When my relative tried to withdraw there were ruffians with bludgeons waiting. He heard a lot of "Hear! Hear!" uttered in unison with the fellow speaking. It was evidently a planted affair. When the atmosphere was quite charged, anyone disagreeing with the speaker was asked to raise his hand. When no one dared to raise a hand, the speaker said that, inasmuch as it was unanimously agreed, all should fill out and sign the volunteer application blank. Thus several hundred employees of the company joined the Volunteer Corps, without even a chance to say goodbye to their families. The same thing was done in banks, commercial houses, societies and associations and schools.

The Communists also made up searching parties composed of the Red Youth Alliance members, the police and army men, and at about two or three o'clock in the morning made house-to-house searches for young men. I met with such a group one night in the following way.

It was a humid warm night. About two o'clock there was loud knocking on the door, as if it was going to be broken down, accompanied by a demand to open it. Simultaneously the sound of the footsteps of four or five men in the vestibule was heard. My wife urged me to go over the back wall and run. While I hesitated, shots were fired and we heard cries of "Hurry up, open the door; if you don't, we'll shoot." I opened the door and two Red soldiers with burp guns and two youth organization men came into the room. "Why didn't you open the door quickly, eh?" they asked with rolling eyes. My cool thinking and self-respect returned. The two soldiers made a minute search of the house and asked whether I had any arms or short-wave radio or any reactionaries in hiding. Then they asked, "Why have you not yet volunteered, why are you in hiding?" I explained that I was suffering from lung trouble and hemorrhoids.

"What is your occupation?"

"I am a teacher in the Korea University."

"Ah, then you are a teacher in Sung-Su Kim's University. Anyway Comrade looks like a reactionary. . . ." A sneering smile was on the face of the Red soldier. At that moment one of the youth organization men looked at me with keen attention, and bringing the candle close to my face, said, "Are you not Professor Kun-Ho Lee of the Korea University? I am a student in T. University. Of course, you would not know me, but I know you well by reading your book." The Red soldier witnessing this seemed to be flabbergasted and then he hit the shoulder of the Youth Member and said, "He is Comrade's teacher?" The former student sent the other soldiers outside and then said to me, "I had been preparing to take the higher civil service examination and had been studying your lectures on Criminal Law, and that is how I got to know your name well. Though I have joined the Youth Alliance in order to avoid the Volunteer Corps, I, also, have much agony. The fact is that you were to have been impressed for the Volunteer Corps tonight. If possible, you had better leave Seoul."

I was so grateful to this student whom I had never seen before that I took a firm grasp of his hand and gave him a bit of advice concerning his future. I said, "It is only a question of time when the Communist army is going to be destroyed. Do not cooperate with them too much. You will take that examination in law by next summer; believe in what I say." He said he understood and added that he would also escape to the country shortly.

Luckily I got through that night, but that did not mean that the danger was over. All kinds of rumors were in circulation. The following day my cousin came just before the curfew hour. He was short of breath and whispered into my ear, "Kim Il Sung is said to have surrendered unconditionally. About tomorrow the American army is going to land at Inchon and disarm the Communists." I was half in belief and half in doubt, but very happy. There were whisperings among the women of the neighborhood. My wife was jubilant also and was eagerly waiting. But several days passed and there was no news about the American army. It was not the first time that we had such an experience. It was due to wishful thinking prompted by anxieties.

The violence of the Reds about the middle of August was such that for me to remain in Seoul looked impossible. One day a certain person came to see me. My wife told him that I was not at home. He said that he was a friend of mine and had come to advise me to go with him to join the Volunteer Corps. I could hear him quite well from where I was hiding. In this manner many were taken to the slaughter ground. I heard afterwards from Professor Y. that a student who had studied under me and was attached to the Political Security Bureau made up many charges against me as a reactionary, trying to have me arrested.

I decided to go into hiding in a country relative's house. The place was about ten miles from Seoul. To cross the Han River was a problem. I started out immediately at the end of the curfew hour, carrying a bundle. To leave behind my wife and four children was indeed hard. My wife told me not to worry about the family but to take care of myself. I could not look up. What would they eat, and how would they fare under these fearful oppressions? I was of no help even when I was at home. I broke loose from these weak feelings and set out. It seemed like a last goodbye, and I looked back again and again. I walked on toward Mapo ferry. On this day the U.N. air force poured down rocket shells and machine-gun bullets. I was sure that no civilian would be hit on purpose, but in the bombing of military installations civilians were harmed.

When I got to the crest of Ahyon-Dong there were fifty or sixty American prisoners of war going toward the city, guarded by Reds with burp guns. How many hundred miles had they walked in that condition? Their bodies were emaciated, there was not one who was not lame, their clothes were tattered and nearly all were without shoes. Some wore only shorts. Those who could not walk were being carried on the shoulders of their buddies. These men, in order to save us from the Communists, had left their homeland and in this foreign land had fought a brave fight. I felt the piercing sensations of gratitude and regret. There was no way of expressing it, but the hearts of the civilians spoke silently, "Don't be angry with us for not having any outward expression. Please preserve your health and wait for the day of our victory." In sadness I moved on. At that hour the thing I felt with certainty was that the American prisoners of war were my countrymen and that the Communist soldiers were my enemies. Fellow-countrymen in spirit are the only fellow-countrymen.

Late in the evening I reached my destination. On the way I was accosted several times by Youth Alliance men and police who questioned and insulted me, but on the whole I had no serious mishap.

What the word "dawai" means or where it originated is not known. However, when the Red soldiers take away the things that belong to others, the civilians say that they have been "dawaied." The word was in wide use during the time when Seoul was occupied by the Red bandits—

many were "dawaied." Immediately after August 15, 1945, when the Soviet soldiers plundered and looted so much, the use of the word was very prevalent.

I, myself, was "dawaied" in the following manner: When the Communist soldiers came into my house they found a medicine case. My wife practiced medicine, but after June 25 we had the signboard removed, though we could not hide the medicine. The expensive medicines we buried underground. As soon as they saw the medicine case they took out cloth from their pockets and put all the medicine and instruments on it. Making up a big bundle, one of them put it on his back in high spirits. But a serious problem arose; one of the bottles marked penicillin contained cholera vaccine. At the time when doctors were getting the last cholera vaccine ration from the Republican government my wife had only the empty penicillin bottles to receive the vaccine in, so the Reds were carrying away cholera vaccine thinking they had penicillin. When we tried to tell them, they would not believe us. Because of the serious consequences that might develop, my wife went after them and finally succeeded in getting them to return it. It was a comedy within a tragedy.

The so-called "commodity tax" is also a form of "dawai." After land reform, a commodity tax of 25 per cent was levied. They say that it is 25 per cent on the year's produce, but the actual determination of the amount of that particular year's produce is made by the so-called "Fact Investigator," a member of the People's Committee of the village. Entirely depending upon what the "Investigator" decides, the 25 per cent can be 35 per cent or 50 per cent or 60 per cent of the actual produce.

The farmers were sick of the land reforms, the "counting the number of beans and peas in each pod, counting the number of pepper plants, etc." But they too were filled with fear. It is not known how far the economic position of the northern farmers has developed after their so-called land reform, but it is certain that their economic strength is less than that of the southern farmers.

The "dawai" of the Reds did not start with the beginning of their defeat, but as soon as they came into Seoul. From government offices, schools, commercial houses and homes they took pianos, sewing machines, furniture and equipment, and shipped them north. Maybe these things were special presents to Stalin. Precious metals were also collected. The Red Women's Alliance members went around saying, "Let us donate precious metals for the sake of the fatherland," and by "fatherland" they meant Russia. At last there was nothing that they did not demand—pepper sauce, bean sauce, spoons, chopsticks, comforts, and finally labor and life itself.

What to eat to sustain life was the biggest problem. The price of rice was 20,000 wons per small mal [approximately ¼ bushel]. Those working for the Reds received special rations and were not concerned with food prices, but the ordinary people were as concerned as with life itself. With what was the food to be bought? There was no income of even a cent, and private possessions were stolen every day. There was nothing to do but to sell anything we could lay our hands on. Daily, people took bundles to the markets to sell for whatever price was offered, and with the proceeds they bought one or two doe [1/10 mal] of rice or barley. Watches, clothing and utensils, one by one, were sold until nothing was left. The next step was peddling, and having no capital, people went into all sorts of small affairs. Selling boiled sweet potatoes, roast beans, tobacco was the prevalent "business." The wife of my friend Professor H. peddled tobacco, and the wife of a director of a business concern peddled plums. My wife had to do similar selling. Men went into hiding in order to avoid arrest and women had to depend on their own wits to live. In spite of everything they could hardly sustain life. When they returned home after spending the whole day on the streets trying to sell their pitiful things, they found new excitement in the form of an order for requisitioned labor. Thus women wept, but weeping did not lighten their burdens.

In this turmoil and misery, a new privileged class arose. The women of this new class bought gold and other precious metals. They bought silken goods for their dresses. They bought rice in straw bags. Masking behind a classless society, these Communists are the real exploiters and enemies of the people. Professing to be for the people, they confront the people with dictatorship and tyranny and their own social order.

The sentiment of the people turned more and more to hatred for the invaders and homesickness for the R.O.K. government. It was the only hope. As the naval guns became busier at Inchon, the National army and the U.N. forces were what we saw even in our dreams.

The cruelties the Communists perpetrated just before their defeat were motivated by characteristics of Communism which could no longer be hidden. The Koreans in the south have learned, through personal experience, about the character of the invader including Bolshevism's animalism, sadism, and deception. Communism is not one of those political ideas which can be appraised on the same level with countless others. It is something entirely apart. It is an eternal enemy of the human race.

Look straight at the revealed evil of the Reds. There can be no compromise, no concession. Here is the clear need for battle. We may have to sacrifice everything, but only by winning this battle can we keep alive the hope for man.

Official Conduct and Personnel Policy

Consistent with the detail with which the plans for the occupation were laid was the care and thoroughness with which they were carried out. The story is a complicated and a frightening one. The studied and plausible politeness of the invaders, the completeness of their communications monopoly, the political astuteness of their personnel policy, their devilishly contrived devices of surveillance and self-criticism, their carefully conceived system of rewards and penalties, their long-run plans for institutional reforms—these were the tools for implementing the blueprint. The creation of a satellite state calls for more than just plans, and the actions of the Reds have, tragically enough, always proved more eloquent than their words.

Official Conduct

Despite the foregoing account by Professor Lee and the personal testimony of other survivors, the invaders in general were not ruthless. In fact, even those who had most reason to hate the foes from the North typically reported their conduct courteous and reasonable. When orders were given, the reasons for them were patiently explained. When systematic confiscations of property took place, the new uses to which it was to be put were carefully indicated. When people were arrested it was done apologetically and always in terms of the necessity of locating some "outside" enemy. Although there was a sharp change in this policy toward the end of the occupation, especially when the news of the Inchon landings swept through the capital, the evidence of this usual official behavior pattern of courtesy and plausibility can be seen at several different social and official levels.

The occupying troops and the lesser administrative officials had apparently received strict briefings as to their everyday behavior in contacts with the rank and file of people, either on the streets or in quasi-official situations. Only a few reports indicated behavior on the part of the invaders that was contrary to this consistent politeness and courtesy. It is worth mentioning, however, that much of this official friendliness was recognized for what it really was—a superimposed veneer. A middle-class newspaperman put it this way: "At the beginning of their occupation," he said, "they were very kind to the people, saying that they would embrace all except the reactionaries. They pointed out that the soldiers did not arrest people directly and they did not strike persons on the streets, except some of the guerrillas. It was a well-known fact that they were well trained to win the hearts of the people." An eighteen-year-old student puts it more simply, "We couldn't *really* be friendly with them."

The invaders had evidently been trained to apply a different approach in their dealings with such persons as doctors, businessmen, artists, and other types of leaders who had previously not been tagged for immediate liquidation. Two courses apparently were followed. In some instances summary trial was held by the People's Court and the defendant either freed or spirited away with little or no publicity. In the majority of cases, however, the Reds were only too glad to give the accused "another chance." To be sure, the pressure to cooperate was great, but the typical story indicates that the arguments were reasonably assembled and that the much-feared and widely rumored systems of torture seldom materialized.

Finally, in dealing with the public at large through official channels, action was seldom taken without a well-reasoned explanation. When the radios were confiscated in July they were avowedly needed for military purposes. Pianos were "required" for hospitals and military rest centers. Sewing machines were to be shipped to factories engaged in the production of emergency clothing for refugees. A doctor's wife summed up the situation: "Whenever quilts, utensils, and other goods were collected, they said they were for the army camps or were to be sent to the front. They said that these things didn't have to be contributed. But no one dared refuse." (The formalized aspect of this official line of behavior is perhaps nowhere better seen than in the various labels attached to the voluntary agricultural contributions—the Rice of Gratitude to the North Korean People's Army, the Rice of Construction for a Better Korea, the Rice of Education, etc.)

It must be pointed out, however, that no amount of superficial courtesy or correct behavior was able to remove the terror of the secret police, the haunting fear of constant surveillance, or the knowledge of the liquidation lists which were used efficiently and ruthlessly.

Apparently the deliberately conceived pattern of correct official behavior paid large dividends not only in terms of the efficiency of the occupation's activities but also in terms of the stereotyped images of the Communist and his motivations. Even when it became apparent to the North Korean forces that they were going to have to leave Seoul and when all of the brutality and the ruthlessness of the invaders were unleashed, eyewitness accounts of the mass murder and public tortures tended not to blame Communism or the system, but rather to explain them as the actions of frustrated men who had temporarily been driven insane. As one young housewife put it: "At first, they were somewhat friendly to people, and it was only as the tide of war turned against them, especially after the United Nations forces landed at Inchon, that they turned into devils doing every savagery."

The last hours of Red Seoul were full of murder, pillage, arson, and frenzy. Even when the citizens of Seoul escaped the anger or the avarice of the fleeing Communists, their stories are still sad with the helplessness and frustration of those hours. For example, here is an account by Kyu-Sik Kim,* a former banker of Seoul. Like most people in the city he was trying to escape the violence of the occupation's end. For three months he had been confined to his home, but now was trying to go to a small nearby town. He came out on a late September afternoon and looked around his neighborhood:

> Carrying a bundle and letting my boy walk in front of me I came out on the street for the first time in three months and after a long illness. My legs were shaky and I found it difficult to walk.
>
> One step, two steps. As I came down from the Namsan area I saw that the whole neighborhood in three months'

* Kyu-Sik Kim's story was one of the collection of stories printed in Seoul after the occupation.

time had been reduced to rubble and the old landmarks could not be made out. How had it happened that Seoul had come to this? My eyes were filled with tears.

I tried to pick the road that was least congested to get to Kyedong. In trying to cross the wooden bridge between Chang-Kyo and Kwang-Kyo we found the road blocked by a crowd of refugees, men and women, old and young, milling and pushing.

At the bridge there was a puppet, scarcely weaned from his mother's breast, holding a gun and flying about saying, "Why don't you stay home? Why are you going crazy like this? Is it because you are happy to see the planes of the American imperialists?" He was wild.

Helplessly we went down to Chang-Kyo, but the scene there was the same. I thought that I had unwittingly come out, got caught, and could not go back, so I squatted down in a dim place on the side of the alley.

The bombing was most severe in the Namsan neighborhood while I sat there. An hour later the puppet soldier was so fagged out and wilted, he couldn't stop the crowd from surging across the bridge, so I wedged myself in between them and crossed too.

Personnel Policy

In establishing the new political hierarchy and in assembling the personnel necessary to run the South Korean state from Seoul, the Communist government followed a policy which might be described in the following terms.

Replace the old leaders. It was an almost invariable rule of the Communists that no pre-Communist leader was to be trusted. No chances were taken with the possible emergence of a counter-elite. Some effort was apparently made to win over a few of the old leaders, but most of them got the word and fled before the invaders came.

Locate and remove poor risks among the rank and file. Some of these, for example the Seoul police, were suspect because of the nature of the job they had been doing. Others were suspect because they were related to an R.O.K. official or officer. Still others were suspect because of their own actions.

As the personal narratives throughout this volume indicate, a most intensive and thorough job was done in locating and eliminating these "poor risks." These narratives could be documented a thousandfold. For example, a Seoul mother told us how she walked around the city during the occupation "trying to find the body of my policeman son. Near the East Gate police station there were piles of dead bodies of R.O.K. police and soldiers covered with rice-straw sacks. I was very careful that nobody would become suspicious of me, for then the Reds watched everyone who came to examine the dead."

Put tried and tested Communists into all positions of real authority. Although South Korean puppets were sometimes used in big-name positions, the real channels of authority were invariably controlled by Party members, many of them imported from North Korea or from Russia.

Encourage and reward technicians and other persons with talents valuable to the state. These included among others physicians and engineers, who represented scarcities in the personnel table, and who were encouraged as warmly as possible to continue work in their specialties.

Open the door to all other workers who express a will-

ingness to cooperate and are not otherwise marked for punishment. To the great majority of workers, the Communists opened the doors freely in return for promise of cooperation.

When the North Koreans entered Seoul, almost all the leaders of the city and state had fled. Many of the police had gone; others were seized and shot. Many other persons, for whom the invaders had well-prepared dossiers, were arrested, usually between midnight and three o'clock in the morning. For example, the chief supervisor of the Ministry of Education was seized at his home shortly after midnight of June 28, taken to a police station, questioned at length from a well-prepared file, questioned again next day from the same file, held for many days, until finally he managed to escape and hide. A number of anti-Communist lawyers were arrested and held for months. It was thought that they were kept for a time in Seoul, and then moved from place to place every night so that their whereabouts would not become known. A very large number of persons simply disappeared and have never been heard from.

But the great majority of the people of the city were approached in a friendly manner by the invaders, told to go back to work, and asked to cooperate. At first no action was taken against those who went back to work, but the government's hold on them gradually tightened. They were told to go to the local police station and "confess" within two weeks. Many of them—those who worked in the ministries, educational institutions, or other "thought-control" agencies—were asked to submit political biographies and make self-criticisms. The screening system operated side by side with the training system, and both were efficient. The important point is that the Communist government operated swiftly and carefully to prepare even the rank and file of its labor force. The sheep were separated from the goats and rewarded with economic preferment and then given further indoctrination to make them even more sheep-like. For the goats there were other methods. The plan was to have as many sheep and as few goats as possible.

Here is a physician's account of how the system operated in his case:

> I was a teacher in the hospital of a medical college and also practiced medicine. The coming of the Communists meant that I found myself very busy. It was not that the number of patients coming to see me increased, it was because my hospital was turned into a field hospital for the North Korean army. Not only was my burden at the hospital increased, but I lost a lot of time because they kept calling me out of my office for meetings. Every day the doctors had to meet for a "cultural hour" when someone read the newspapers aloud or a speech by Stalin or Molotov or Kim Il Sung, or when we were called upon to report on Communist literature we had read. There was no specifically announced punishment for the absentee, but we were in constant fear of it, and therefore attended diligently.
>
> To tell the truth, the R.O.K. army was so powerless, and the victory of the North Korean army was so overwhelming, that people were not disinclined to work diligently for the invaders. We could not help but feel bitterly about the Rhee government for abandoning its citizens without any notice. At the hospital, every member of the staff worked hard and automatically. We organized a People's Committee, and elected a chairman

who had been known as a leftist, but physicians of lower rank or nameless underlings sprang forth to occupy the important positions.

It seemed that the army did not intend to interfere with the personal or medical affairs of the hospital, except in respect to cooking and finance. But responsible officials called cultural officers became very important. They interfered with staff classes, and gave orders to the front men in the hospital.

Though there was a group of non-Communist doctors, they could not hold important positions. They would have been afraid to hold them, anyway, because that would have meant contact with the Communist leaders and trouble. I worked at the hospital until the end of the occupation, and every night when I returned home I was so tired I could only fall right in bed.

I think I was under constant supervision. I dared not converse freely with other people. When we talked we were on guard against each other.

My greatest worry was that they might take me to North Korea. But on August 20, when the hospital was ordered to move northward, doctors, nurses, medical students, and other staff members being threatened with death if they did not go, I escaped and lived underground.

The most important personnel work of the occupation government during the first weeks in Seoul, however, was in tightening its hold on positions of authority, and the key to this operation was imported personnel. When the invasion took place, the North Korean government was ready with a cadre estimated variously at three to seven thousand persons, who were to come in with the troops or shortly afterwards and take over the key jobs. There is evidence that this group had been selected and trained very carefully, and that their preparation had begun long before the invasion.

Some were merely personnel moved from North Korean jobs to take over similar jobs in Seoul, for example the top public information and radio personnel. Others were South Koreans, who had been taken up to North Korea several years before the invasion and prepared for their new jobs, for example the new South Korean Minister of Education, who had been principal of a girls' high school until he went to North Korea in 1947. Still others, who were neither South Korean in origin nor members of North Korean ministries, had been specially trained in the North for specific types of jobs, for example the Seoul police force, which came down to take over the city from the North Korean troops a few days after the invasion. Some of these policemen, with commissions predating the invasion, reported that they had been waiting on the 38th parallel for several days before the troops moved.

There is ample evidence also of Russian training in this cadre. The man appointed police chief in Seoul, for example, was a North Korean who had been a major in the Russian army. The chief engineer of the Seoul radio station had been trained in Moscow.

In general, the policy was to fill positions of executive responsibility and positions of special trust from this imported cadre. It was said that in the ministries, positions down to section chiefs were filled by men well and favorably known to Kim Il Sung. Sometimes, however, in the preliminary stages South Korean collaborators took over to be superseded later by personnel previously trained and imported for the job. Here is an employee's account of how it was done.

> On June 28, we were talking in the basement of my office in a state of half-belief when Chung [a collaborator] turned up drunk and shouting loudly, "Long live the People's Republic!" He shook our hands and embraced us. We had not hung up the flag of the People's Republic and he asked us to put it up immediately; but nobody could draw it because we had never seen it. I wondered how such an amiable fellow could turn into a scared wolf overnight. He said his father had just been released from the prison in which the R.O.K. had confined him for being a deputy of North Korea. He ordered us to call up all of the employees to set up a Self-Government Committee. I don't know why we were so discouraged that we could not refuse him, but the Self-Government was organized that afternoon. Chung named himself chief of the inspection and liaison section, so that he could watch our activity. He insisted on driving our curator out of committee membership, mostly to restrain the majority of us who were supporting the curator.
>
> From that day, pale Party members began to stream into the office, carrying carbine rifles and Japanese swords, for meetings with Chung. On June 29, Chung himself came in with a carbine and sword. Thereafter we were continually called to meetings.
>
> On July 5, a haughty young man appeared and asked where the curator's office was. He went into the office and sitting in the curator's chair he introduced himself to us. He announced that he had been dispatched from the Korean Material Civilization Relics Investigation and Preservation Group belonging directly to the cabinet of the People's Republic, and that his main purpose was to take over all museums, galleries, and palaces throughout

South Korea. He bade us to get prepared because he was going to take up his business immediately.

Next morning he came with a couple of scoundrels to chase us out of our offices and seal the office rooms and library, as if we were thieves. Nothing remained but picks, shovels, and sickles. All of us, regardless of rank, had to clean the entire building.

We were forced to work on Sunday and two hours longer each day. For one hour before the opening of the office we had to read newspapers, for one hour at noon we had to learn songs, and for another hour after the office closed we were obliged to attend lectures. We had no free time. Nor did we have any salary and thus suffered from want of food.

We were frequently turned out for meetings. These meetings invariably passed unanimous resolutions, offering our money and labor. They put us under surveillance continually. They required us to submit the project of the day, the month, the year, and individual diaries, even notes taken at the lecture or reading meetings. Besides, they sometimes demanded our whole night's work at the ammunition factories. They imposed so many things that we could never meet the demand even if we worked three times as much as possible. What my fate would have been if I had refused to obey them was all too clear to me.

The more severe the air raids became, the more irritable they became. They ordered us to disperse the articles exhibited in the museum; they so forced us to work that we could scarcely find any time to sleep day or night; and they constantly reminded us that we were always under watch. We had no freedom of any kind. As the occupation drew near a close, they would suddenly appear at our homes at any time of night. We spent the last few days in the basement in tension and terror. Just before the U.N. forces entered Seoul they ran away in a hurry without a word.

The North Koreans came in also with full and reliable information about those South Koreans whom they could expect to trust in important jobs. Prominent among these were the pre-invasion Communists, who came crawling out of the underground to claim their rewards when the first North Korean guns began to boom near Seoul. Approximately two per cent of the school teachers had been denied employment by the R.O.K. government because of their Communism, but now this group quickly became masters of the destiny of their fellow teachers, in charge of hiring and firing. Similarly, in any village whoever had been the secretary of the Communist Party was likely to become its most powerful citizen. He was instrumental in designating the mayor to be appointed, and together with the mayor he appointed the Land Division Committee.

Who were these pre-invasion South Korean Communists? Evidence suggests that economically they were more likely to be middle or upper class than lower class, that they were most likely to be over thirty, and that only a comparatively small number of them were in jail at the moment of invasion. Many were in hiding, but there were many others who still occupied respected positions (doctors, lawyers, executives, public officials) giving no hint of their Communist activities and convictions.

During the occupation these pre-war Communists were more likely to be major influences in smaller villages than in Seoul, where the real power was retained by the North Korean imports. In fact, there is more than a suggestion that many of the Seoul Communists were objects of good-natured humor from their northern fellows, and that they were gradually eased out in favor of better officeholders.

Technicians, of course, were important in the Communist scheme of things and every effort was made to retain these men in their jobs. When the occupation ended, an attempt was made to take as many technical men as possible to North Korea.

There were also local puppets. In a number of organizations and bureaus, it was the policy to appoint a safe front man to the nominal top job, while the real power was kept resident in a second man. The real power in the Ministry of Communications, for example, lay in a vice-minister who had been trained in Russia. In many districts and villages it was not the mayor who held the real power, but someone on the People's Committee. So the pattern of secret authority expressed itself.

An important plank in the Communist platform gave women an equal chance with men to do jobs for which they were qualified. This applied not only to political appointments (almost always a woman was appointed to the People's Committee) but also to business and industrial jobs, desk or manual work. In Seoul, however, although the lines of development were laid down, there was too little time to develop this labor source very fully.

The long hand of Communist personnel planning reached everywhere, from the positions of leadership down even to the children and the vagrants. When it became clear that Seoul would have to be abandoned, the Communists gave the children and vagrants of the city several days' instructions in how to set fires and demolish buildings; at a city dumping ground they were allowed to practice with gasoline "fire sticks." And they were paid in advance for the job they were to do. It was these children and the derelicts who set fire to many of Seoul's finest buildings when the North Korean armies marched out.

Chul-Hoe Koo

Treatment of "Reactionaries"

Chul-Hoe Koo is one of Korea's best-known newspaper reporters.

About 6:30 in the afternoon of August 12 while I sat on the veranda porch with my wife, someone called outside the gate. Thinking it was a friend, I stepped out and found a man around thirty years old, wearing khaki uniform and high red boots, with a pistol in a case slung over his shoulder. I recognized him as one of the puppets but it was already too late to retreat, so pretending innocence I asked him whom he wanted to see.

He twisted his lips in a smile and countered with "Are you Mr. Koo?" I admitted I was and invited him to come in. Paying no attention to the invitation, he announced that he was from the Chongno Internal Affairs [Police] Office.

"You were a candidate for National Assemblyman?" he asked.

"Yes."

"And Chief of Political and Economics Bureau of the H News?"

"That's right."

"And yet you have not surrendered?" he persisted, and I simply said "No." He then said that he had further questions to ask and told me to accompany him. I said I had lung trouble and could not walk far, but when he assured me that I could come back immediately I had no alternative but to follow him. My wife, realizing what it meant, hastily wrapped up 1,000 wons and some medicine and slipped them to me. As I started to follow the puppet she ran after us with tearful entreaties. When we reached the corner and she could no longer see us, he started to put handcuffs on me. I said quickly, "Comrade! Put your mind at ease. I will follow you as a gentleman." He hesitated a moment then brusquely ordered me to walk ahead of him. When we came to the police station, instead of going in I was told to cross the street. I was immediately suspicious. "*This* is the Chongno Station; where are we going?" In an angry voice he told me to keep still and do as I was told. Like a person in a trance I went the way of darkening roads and arrived at the Central Internal Affairs Office.

In the vestibule everything was in total darkness, probably because of the air-raid blackout. Holding me by my coat my guard led me to a large corner room on the second floor. The windows were hung with black curtains and there were many desks with candles on them. About ten young men sat listlessly on a long bench near the entrance. Here and there in front of desks men with bowed heads were being examined in an atmosphere surcharged with tension.

He told me to sit in a chair in front of his desk; then he took out a meal ticket and ordered food. When white rice and beef soup were brought in he ordered them to be placed before me and, prompted by some unknown reason, in a kindly manner he asked me to eat. For a month and a half I had had no white rice and meat soup, and I ate with great relish. When I had finished I took out my 1,000 wons and asked him how much the meal cost. "Capitalism rooted in the bones!" he sneered. "In our People's Republic we treat even reactionaries like you with humanity."

At that very moment one of the examiners jumped to

his feet and repeatedly slapped the young man he was questioning, shouting, "Tell the truth. How many patriots have you sentenced to death?" and kicked him in the chest. The young man groaned, but denied that there was a single case, which won him another kick. Judging by the drift of the questions that followed, the young man must have been a judge advocate in the Republican navy.

Just then we heard the air-raid sirens and the sentries below shouted in hoarse voices to put out the lights. In the darkness each examiner took his prisoner to what was evidently supposed to be a safer place. I was taken to the second-floor hall. My examiner pointed to a long wooden bench and told me to sleep on it. Then he spread a blanket over a table and lay down himself. But I could not go to sleep for a long while.

In the morning I was taken back to the room of the Security Police for the regular examination.

"You were a candidate in the May 30 election and have been Chief of the Political and Economic Bureau of a reactionary paper, and yet instead of surrendering, you went in hiding. This proves you are loyal to the Republic of Korea and an evil element." With the same sort of reasoning the examiner tried to fix upon me the crime of "reactionaryism" and of being a "traitor to the nation." As the questioning became sharper, I tried to give them as little information as possible. All around me I could hear the sound of slapping and kicking and charges and denials.

Hours later my examiner took me down to the basement where he wrote up the document on my case. Breakfast had been skipped, but after a while we were given a ball of bean and barley and a chestnut-size doen-jang [bean cheese of salty taste]. Suddenly, while we were eating, an examiner got up and savagely slapped the face of the man next to me. "Aren't you going to tell the truth, you scoundrel?" he yelled. To everyone's surprise the suspect sprang to his feet and shouted back angrily:

"I eagerly worked in the All-Nation Committee of the Federation of Labor [a leftist organization] ever since the August 15 Liberation. I was arrested by them [meaning the Republic of Korea] and suffered almost to death; I was subjected to the Alliance for Protection and Guidance [a re-orientation organization for leftists]. Yet I have continued to fight for the destruction of the Republic of Korea. Do you strike persons in the People's Republic also? We heard that in the People's Republic a man is subject to three years of hard labor for slapping another's face, yet you strike me who have until now fought for the People's Republic?"

In his excitement he grew short of words and wept aloud. The fellow who struck him seemed at first to be flabbergasted, and for a moment he stood still and looked at the man with his bloodshot eyes. Then he pounced on him and, striking him again, said, "This scoundrel is not yet in his right mind! Do you want to see what it's like? Get down on your knees, you scoundrel!" He kicked and trampled the knees of the man, until unable to bear any more he groaned and begged for mercy.

The Political Security man who had charge of me took the document he had prepared and hurried me to a basement room with Japanese straw mats on the floor.

There he turned me over to the Division Chief, who merely glanced at me and said, "Now who is this scoundrel? Wait a little outside the door." He took me outside and made me stand in the hallway. Then, taking a piece of wire about three yards long, he went back into the darkened examination room and shut the door. All my attention focused on that room and the terrible cries of pain coming from it. Evidently they bound the suspect with wire and beat him with a bludgeon. I could hear the voice of his torturer shouting: "How many men have you killed, you scoundrel? Do you still deny that as a police officer you did not kill our patriots?" (These Political Security officers always used "this scoundrel" and "that scoundrel" when examining anyone.)

About twenty minutes later the door opened, and the chief examiner emerged, dragging the blood-soaked young man and calling to a uniformed officer to put him in a prison cell. When I looked inside the room I saw the blood-covered wire and a knotty oaken bludgeon lying there in the middle of the floor as if waiting for the next victim. The torturer seemed to be worn out as he leaned sideways against the back of a chair and drew deeply on a cigarette.

A moment later he crushed the cigarette and told me to come in. I dragged my shaking legs into the room and stood close to him. "Why did you not surrender? Evil elements like yourself, I say, cannot be forgiven," he threatened, yet in an ordinary tone of voice. He turned over some pages of the document brought in by the other investigator, asking a few questions; then he gave me a pen and some sheets of paper and told me to write down all the things I had done. After that he asked the man in the next room to watch me and went to get his lunch.

It was lucky for me that he left, for while he was gone I hurriedly read the document that he had left lying there and wrote mine along the same lines but in a way that would be more favorable to me.

About an hour later he returned. One after the other he read the first document and the one I had written, making comparisons. Then under my document he wrote, "Opposed Trusteeship, Chief of Political Economic Bureau of a reactionary newspaper, Candidate at National Assembly Election, a Christian Believer."

Looking hard at me he said, "You are being turned over to the Preliminary Court, I want you to know that." He wrote an imprisonment order and called an officer in uniform. Having had a fear of being tortured, this sudden turn of affairs was very welcome, and with lighter steps I followed the officer to the culture house [prison].

At the culture house I was led to room No. G. There were over ten men in the room, and in the darkness they looked like bears in a cage. As I came in and sat down a young man came close just as if I were a friend from a distant place and asked how it happened I was there. Not knowing who or what he was I avoided telling him then. Shortly afterwards I learned that the prisoners here were mostly police officers, members of Home Guards, Korean Youth Organization and City Ward officials, and refugees from the north. And there were others: one got caught while listening to a short-wave radio, another had smoked on the second story and was suspected of having given signals to the air raiders, and there was even a member of the Alliance for Protection and Guidance who had probably expected to become a Red leader.

After a while the short-wave young man came close to me and, indicating with his eyes a young man sitting nearby, said in a whisper, "Be careful. That man is a member of the Communist Youth Alliance. He is on friendly terms with the Instructor [prison guard] and you must be very careful."

Soon the usual supper of a ball of barley and beans and a little bean cheese was brought in. No one spoke a word for fear of being punished by the Instructor. The air raid continued all night long and with the raid, the mosquitoes, and fleas there was little chance of sleep.

The next morning I heard several prisoners express a wish to be "turned over" as soon as possible. When I asked them what they meant they told me they wanted to be sent to the City Political Security Bureau, located in the National Library. A person with political affiliations like me could be clearly judged a criminal, they said. Therefore, I might be "turned over" even today. Their crimes, on the other hand, depended upon what confessions could be beaten out of them and torture was all they could look forward to. One of them, a member of the Korean Youth Organization [rightist], was still in command of his courage. He said, "If we are going to be beaten to death, there is no help for it. A few days before I got caught I saw about 300 U.N. prisoners of war passing at Eulji Road and shed real tears. They wore no clothes as such, no shoes, and they looked like walking corpses, tall figures with their bellies sunken to their backs so that their waists looked like the quarter moon and their sunken eyes made them look like ghosts. I can see them even now. Maybe it was because they were so thin, but I wondered why their arms were hanging so long. When our friends who fought for us suffered like that, let come what may to us. If we are going to die, we die; if we are going to live, we live." Then, turning completely around in his seat, he suddenly clenched his two fists and was seized with a fit of trembling. The leftist Youth Alliance man next to him watched the scene with strange eyes.

During the day I was transferred to the so-called City Political Security Bureau and was taken to a third-floor office of the Seoul Price Goods Company which was being used as a culture house. The day was warm and humid, and as I entered I saw around two hundred men sitting on the floor crowded together like bean sprouts in an earthen jar, and the heat and stench of perspiration stabbed my nostrils and choked me.

It was the middle of August and the heat was at its height. Everyone was thirsty and wanted water and only water. But the water ration was one cup to each prisoner three times a day. Even this was not always possible for lack of organization. Meals came twice a day, one near nine in the morning and the other about nine in the evening, each a ball of barley sprinkled with salt. Withstanding hunger, not a few will swap this barley for the water that comes afterward. For the first time I discovered that hunger is hard to bear but burning thirst is far worse. To get any sleep in a place like this is also an agony in itself.

One day the class leader [one of the prisoners assigned to carry food and water] changed, and I was the lucky one to receive the high honor of appointment. Everyone tried hard to be that dignitary because then he could drink all the water he wanted. One of the prisoners remarked that he would not have a further wish even in death than to fill himself with water. When I went out to the pump I drank about half a bucket of muddy water, scarcely noticing two earthworms squirming at the bottom of the bucket. After that, out of some sort of a guilty conscience, I tried my very best to do equal justice to everyone in the room in doling out water.

On August 18, after a brief examination, I was sent across the street to the culture house in the compound of the National Library. I remembered my fellow prisoners who had wanted to be "turned over" to this place, where they had told me you could even smoke if you wanted to. I soon found out that they need not have envied me. This place was in reality much worse. The Instructor in charge was an evil one who freely emphasized his insults with a square-edged bludgeon even on those who just wanted to drink or to make water. Once while I was in there I saw an old man fold a piece of paper, make a cup of it, and use it to drink his own water. When someone asked how the taste was, the corners of his lips twitched weakly, "What else?"

On August 20, toward sunset, I was transferred to the West Gate Culture House [West Gate Prison]. Detention House No. 1, Cell No. 10, second floor, was my allotted abode. The capacity of the room was twenty persons. Besides two who had been candidates at the May 30 election, there were three public officials, a Dong [a section of the city] chief, a member of the Korean Youth Organization, a migrant from the north, a member of the Alliance for Protection and Liquidation, an employee of the American Embassy, a pastor, an editor of a weekly, and others.

On August 24 the air raid was very severe during the whole day, and Pastor Yun-Sil Kim winked and whispered, "Perhaps they have landed at Inchon." For a moment I could not control my joy. But several days passed and there was no news, no change.

At the beginning of September there were already over eight thousand patriots imprisoned here. This meant that a large portion of the pre-invasion leaders in Seoul who had not been able to escape or stay in hiding had been dragnetted. The members of the National Assembly, officers of political parties, university professors, judiciary officials, administrators, army and police officers, city section officials, members of staffs of the Korean Youth Organization and of the Home Guards, literary men, newspaper men, religious leaders, artists, etc., were all included. These useful citizens had helped to create the truly democratic political authority, the Republic of Korea, which the nations of the world have recognized, but this fact was now their crime. Most of these people had been arrested through informers, and their families never knew whether they were alive or dead.

I was suffering with an abscess on the back and diarrhea, and I was extremely weak. Whenever the prison physician came on his rounds friends put in kind words, and eventually he recorded mine as a special, serious case. On September 3 I was removed with Pastor Yun-Sil Kim to the infirmary.

Lying down on the floor, covered with a dirty blanket and carrying on a conversation in a low voice is a blessing which only a sick prisoner in an infirmary is allowed. There were thirty persons in the ward, nearly half of whom had tuberculosis. The others were gastric or surgical cases. I was on the west side of the hallway with Mr. Sang-Ik Lee of the J newspaper and Pastor Kim.

We were patients in name only and rarely received any medical care. One or two dropped out every day. Pastor In-Sun Chun, who was suffering from cancer, could not swallow even a spoonful of water, and Pastor Kim, in spite of his own illness, attended him most assiduously, but he soon answered the call of the Lord. Pastor Kim broke a wisp of Pastor Chun's hair, and bits of his fingernails and toenails, using his own fingernails to do it, and wrapped them in a piece of paper to save to give to Pastor Chun's family. He also took a piece of underwear Pastor Chun had died in, shook it out for many hours to get rid of all the lice—some of them as big as a grain of barley—and put it with the other things for possible future delivery. Then we carried Pastor Chun's body with prayers to the mortuary.

In the near-dawn of September 15, Newspaperman Lee, Pastor Kim, Yung-Sup Choo—a hometown friend of mine—and I were lying side by side and looking out to the eastern edge of the sky where the sun was rising. From the yew tree outside the window a magpie shouted. Mr. Lee touched my shoulder and said, "Good omen!"

In the evening Mr. Choo was called away to be examined, but he returned after only an hour. When we asked him why he was back so soon, he told us that when they entered the examining room the prosecutors were running about busily and paid no attention to them. After a while they said they had to go to a meeting and told them to come back later. While they were waiting Mr. Choo met a friend, arrested only a few days ago, who told him that he had heard on the short-wave radio that on September 9 our National army and the U.N. forces had landed at Wolmi Island in Inchon Harbor, and on the 12th they had landed at Ongjin. "Now it's happening, isn't it?" he had cried out excitedly. That night we could not sleep.

About eleven in the forenoon of September 16, seven or eight of the investigators and prosecutors of the City Political Security Bureau rushed in to make a hurried check on the names, crimes, experiences, etc., of all the patients in the infirmary. They asked each one if he could walk 25 miles, 20 miles, 15 miles on the road. They implied that these questions were being asked to determine who were to be sent out for the harvesting of crops. This was a temptation to the young and those not seriously ill. But four of us, because of what we had heard the previous night about the Inchon landing, tried to dissuade them from trying to go. In order to save as many as possible, through Chosun Christian University student Yang I sent a mouth-to-mouth message to certain key men in the room. My message must have taken effect, because the first two or three on the list said that they could not walk more than two or three miles—one even claimed that he could not go outside the gate—and the rest, taking the cue, said that they, too, could not walk the proposed distances. The investigators hurriedly made their records and went to the next room. Until deep in the night we heard them calling out numbers and there was much confusion. We did not know what was going on or for what reason, but two days later, the cleaner (a prisoner) told us that the cells were nearly half empty. Yet I could not believe that several thousand prisoners could be transferred in the short space of two days.

On September 20 the rumble of gunfire was continuous but it was hard to believe that it came from a friendly army. All night long the firing continued and the air-raid sirens did not stop.

The next morning we saw puppet soldiers, with tree branches on their heads, climbing the mountain behind the prison toward Hong-jewon. Everyone in the room was nervous. Yang asked me what I thought we had better do. He thought perhaps the room should have a leader so that if something developed suddenly, we could take unanimous action.

But Newspaperman Lee did not think such a plan would work. "Even if we did succeed in breaking out," he said, "we would have puppet soldiers to face outside and the armed Instructors inside. What can the few of us do against so many?" Then he told us he had discovered a secret hole to the ceiling and we decided we would hide there when necessary until the situation improved enough for us to escape.

About ten o'clock in the morning the Political Security Bureau men, followed by the Instructor, again hastily checked the names of the prisoners, their crimes and experiences. Not more than ten minutes after they had left a big uproar started in the prison yard. We all stood close to the bars and looked down on the yard. A crowd of blue-clad convicts and white-clad prisoners were running this way and that trying to avoid volleys of bullets pouring into them. We thought it was an attempted escape. We too yelled and kicked at the door, but it was too strong for such weak patients. Just then we saw two young men running in the alley behind the Infirmary and asked them to help us. They stopped, picked up a big rock, and smashed the doors for us. We shouted and rushed out. But the unrelenting Instructors ran toward us from the yard, brandishing guns. Without hesitation we went back to the room and everyone covered himself completely with a blanket. The Instructors came in shooting and ordered us not to move. All were as silent as dead rats. Then, inside for a moment everything was quiet; we thought perhaps the Instructors had gone after the fleeing prisoners.

The uproar in the yard continued for a while; and then from outside we heard the voices of the Instructors call out in a tone of compromise: "Everyone gather at the detention house. Gather in orderly manner at the detention house." It sounded suspicious, and we decided the time had come to use the hiding place discovered by Lee in the ceiling. It was then we discovered that K. was missing. The hole was full of dust and cobwebs and completely dark, but Pastor Kim, Newspaperman Lee, Mr. Choo and I stayed there until after the noon hour. Then, hoping that the back gate was open, we came down from the ceiling.

The four of us carefully but quickly started toward the back gate. Unluckily we were seen by the Instructors in the yard. They followed and shot at us. All was lost! We turned around and went back to the ceiling. Quieting our quickened breath Pastor Kim, Mr. Choo and I waited for Lee, but he never returned. Sadness enshrouded us as friends dropped out one by one. Throughout the night we waited, while shells exploded and smashed the surroundings of the prison and the Inwang Mountain. Morning came and still we waited. When the day was more than half gone we could no longer bear the excruciating pains of hunger, and at the risk of being shot Pastor Kim descended to the prison kitchen to get food and to see if he could find out what had happened. Uneasiness overwhelmed us while he was gone, but after about twenty minutes, he came back with a bag on his shoulder.

"How . . .?" we began to ask in unison.

He shook his head and said, "Quit thinking about getting out. When I got to the kitchen, luckily there was no Instructor, only the kitchen hands were there. I begged for some rice and they gave me this with these dried fish as a side dish." He smiled and opened the bag. White rice and dried fish, intended for the Instructors and the puppet soldiers! We ate greedily as Pastor Kim continued:

"I asked them what had happened to those who gathered at the detention house yesterday, but they would not answer. One of them said angrily, 'Hurry and get out of here before you get caught by the Instructor.' So I left them. On my way here, I met an Instructor, and he demanded to know what I was carrying. I told him in a weak and humble manner that it was food for a seriously ill patient, and shrunk away."

We could not endure the cramped hole in the ceiling any longer, so that night we took our courage between our teeth and went down to a room where seven or eight seriously ill patients remained. As the night grew deeper and the cannonade became more and more violent, plaster fell from the ceiling and the walls. Before long a puppet officer came and said, "Comrades, you are sick people, and we are going to take you to the army hospital in the rear. The ambulance will be ready in about an hour." Then he ordered the Instructor to "tie our arms by twos." To our surprise Mr. Choo spoke up: "There is no necessity to incur extra expense for the state. Even if we are not released until tomorrow, we will be taken care of in our homes."

"We are taking you to the army hospital to protect you. If we left you here, you may be massacred when the Americans and the remnant National army come." With this the officer turned his electric torch so the Instructor could see to tie our wrists. They left us tied together for about an hour.

The moon had set and it was very dark when heavy leather-shoed footsteps and light from the pocket torches told us that they were returning. They announced that the car was ready and told us to come out. There were seven of them altogether: the officer who had come a while ago, two armed instructors, and four puppet soldiers, also armed. Frightened, one of the patients begged for life. I found my own feet hesitant, and tried a delaying tactic: "Four of us in front can go," I told them, "but the serious cases in the back cannot move." But it didn't work. They ordered us to get going and said they would help any who needed it.

The four of us followed them to the front of an air shelter next to the prison doctor's office where they told us to stand in line. At the next moment without a single word they aimed their guns at us. It was so sudden that as a reflex I fell backward into the dugout. At the split second of my falling my hand was free of the rope (I had worked it while waiting in the ward) and I screened myself where the shelter turns. More shots were fired. Pastor Kim and the young man bound with him lay still. Mr. Choo who had fallen beside me groaned. The soldiers with flashlights looked in, "One scoundrel isn't there," and they fired again. I did not know whether I was hit or not. I held my breath and stood flat against the wall. When it seemed the firing was over I stretched out my hand to Mr. Choo and felt warm sticky blood. Then the sound of shooting came again but from overhead. The beam of a flashlight suddenly touched my knee. I shrank back. But they must have thought we were all dead for they said, "Let's put the rest in and cover them up." They seemed to be going to the infirmary again.

I took a deep breath and felt over my body, but there was no pain, no blood. By a miracle I was alive!

With quiet steps I went to the side of the shelter. There appeared to be no sentries nearby. I saw that the window of the doctor's office was open and climbed to it. As I looked around to find a hiding place the window glass fell out with a crash. I knew that puppet soldiers would be nearby and I started for the detention quarters where I knew the layout. I had almost reached them when I noticed light and human movement. I shrank away to the left. Running, I entered the covered way to the convicts' quarters, fell flat and looked around, but saw no one. Everything was quiet and I could hear only my own breathing.

At the moment gun reports were coming from the infirmary. More massacres. I offered a prayer for my sick friends whose lives I knew were being snuffed out by those gun shots.

All the doors were closed, so I tried to get into an empty oil drum standing in a corner but it was not a good hiding place. Not satisfied, I came out. Just then I heard someone call "Comrade Choo! Have you seen a man going in this direction?" My breath stopped and my whole body trembled. They now knew that one of us had escaped from the air shelter.

Standing outside, pressed flat against the wall, I looked around. There was no place to hide. I felt around and found some luxurious flowering plants at the right-hand corner. I fell flat under them. The fellow who was calling "Comrade Choo" came out from the direction of the cells. The sound of his footsteps came nearer and nearer. Pulling my body backward I looked at the wall on the left. Up to the two-story rooftop it would be more than three human heights. The building on the right side was a one-story house but there was a parapet about a yard high above the eave. I thought to myself, "If I went up there I'd live." Using all the strength I had I made the rooftop and hid behind the parapet. Soon someone, evidently the one who was calling for "Comrade Choo," walked down the flower garden. From the same direction came the indistinct voices of other men.

As day broke I climbed over to a corner on the other side of the roof and lay down. On the west I could see the mountain at the back of the prison, on the right was a screening wall, and above was the branch of an apricot tree covering my head. I stayed there for two nights, not sleeping a wink.

By dawn of September 23 I could no longer stand the thirst. I remembered what I had seen the old man doing in the culture house at the National Library, and I too drank my own water. It was bitter but gave some relief.

The puppets still held the mountain behind the prison. I could hear their machine guns and burp guns popping like soya beans in a frying pan. Suddenly one of them cried out and, startled, I looked up toward the mountain and saw a soldier in deep khaki uniform and steel helmet who looked altogether different from the others. Soon two, then three, and then several of them appeared. They looked for a moment and then I heard the Kyong Sang dialect give an order to fire. I almost went crazy as the rocket shells aimed at the prison buildings exploded. I shut my eyes and prayed to God to save my life.

Since the first line of the National army had come up that hilltop, the tank column must be outside the prison gate. Using all the strength left in my weakened legs, I climbed down to the ground and cautiously walked to a side gate. But the heavy gate was still shut as if nothing had happened, and from the second and third story of the main building gunfire of the puppets continued resistance. In a side door in the wall I found a knothole through which I looked and looked but could not see any tanks.

A fighter plane swooped down and strafed the prison ground; bullets fell like a shower around me, but miraculously I was not hit. From the other side of the wall a machine gun shot at the plane, forcing it to withdraw. Quiet prevailed for a moment, and I went back to the side door to see how things were outside, but there was still no sign of the tanks. Struggling with discouragement I crept back into the flower garden.

Soon the prison was noisy again with gunfire from the burp guns. The puppet soldiers went around strafing anything that looked suspicious. I lay as flat as possible, wishing that the earth would swallow me. The burp gunners passed by and disappeared.

I discovered a pile of wood and started to climb it, but when I was about halfway up, the wood tumbled down and took me along with it. I was panic-stricken for fear the puppet soldiers would discover me, but nothing happened and I crept up again. I dug a hole in the center of the top of the wood pile and made a kind of dugout in which I could hide. I was no sooner finished than four planes thundered over. I covered my head with wood, held a piece in each hand, and offered a prayer. The planes wheeled around. I shut my eyes. The bullets came down like rain. There was a sound like a thunderclap, and I was thrown bodily out on the pile. When I collected myself and looked around me, I saw the building on the roof of which I had spent two days had been hit by a bomb. I then hid in another pile of debris.

The burp guns that strafed between air raids came near again. They were shooting into the wood pile this time. It seemed certain that they suspected I was there. When things were quiet again I looked up, and saw that the wood pile was afire.

Without thinking of the nearby puppets, I jumped

down and ran toward the cells. I entered the cell house that was nearest but it was a shambles from the bombing of yesterday so I decided to hide in the undamaged bathroom. At that moment I heard steps and through the window saw a puppet soldier approaching with a rifle and fixed bayonet. Making as little noise as possible, I entered a room on the opposite side with a "Dark Room, No Admittance" sign on the door. The soldier went into the bathroom and I heard him jabbing his bayonet at random into a stack of empty straw bags standing on one side of the room. Finding nothing, he went toward the cells, but soon returned and looked around once more. Sometime after he left I noticed a reflection of light coming into the darkroom. I opened the door and saw fire. The puppet soldier must have set it before he left.

I started for the infirmary. On the way I discovered a fountain of water caused by a break in a water pipe. I was so delighted that without any thought of caution I drank my fill and felt that I could live now. I reached the infirmary and once more climbed into the hole in the ceiling where we had hidden ourselves before.

Two days later I heard voices of children from the direction of the hospital office. Through a crack I saw three little beggar boys searching for food. I concluded that the puppets had been routed and descended. The children were frightened when they saw my ghost-like figure with sunken eyes and seedy hempen clothes. I waved my hand and said in a reassuring voice.

"Boys, are there many Northern soldiers around?"

"Yes, there are. But who are you, uncle?" I smiled and

said I was a beggar. That put their minds at ease and they told me that outside the gate there were still many of them. Nokponi, beyond Hong-jeiwon (3 to 4 miles), had been liberated by the National army yesterday, and over the mountain there were lots of National army soldiers. "But, say uncle, where is the rice? Which hypo medicine cost the most?" I told them the medicines were in another room and went down to the basement where the medicines were kept, shut the door, and bolted it. I was thirsty and starved, so I broke many vials of vitamin C in an attempt to regain some strength.

All day I remained hidden in the basement. That night, passing the surgery clinics on my way back to the ceiling, my feet kicked something soft and heavy. It was a bag of rice that must have been dropped by the beggar boys. With this welcome present I went back to the basement where I had already seen a charcoal stove and a kettle. I found a basin used for antiseptic solutions and set out to cook some rice.

When I thought that I had everything ready, I realized I had no way to make any fire. I sat down on the cement floor and thought hard until late night and then it came to me—there was a way! Had they not set fire to the wood pile, to the bathroom? I took a piece of absorbent cotton, tore off a piece of cloth from a mattress, and started off. Cautiously watching right and left, I made a thorough search but I could not find any fire. Heartbroken, I was returning when, passing another building that was bombed and burnt, I heard a hissing sound and saw a faint glow. My chest heaved as I went to investigate. The coal tar on a split telephone pole was boiling and burning weakly into the wood. I made a wick with the piece of cloth and lighted it. I covered it with the cotton and kept blowing at it until I got back to the basement. Then I made fire in the charcoal stove, more than half filled the basin with rice, got water from the broken water pipe, and cooked the rice. I ate rice until I could hardly breathe.

Techniques of Thought Control

Seizure of Radio Seoul was the first recorded action of the occupation forces in respect to the communications system. They began at once to broadcast messages to the populace: Your government has fled, the People's Republic is now in control. Go back to your work. Everyone will be forgiven if he goes back to work.

It seems strange that Radio Seoul, which had an output of 35 kilowatts and covered all Korea, should be so immediately available to them. When it became clear that the city could no longer be held, it would seem that good military policy would have dictated its destruction or immobilization by the South Koreans. Possibly the Rhee government, which broadcast a fighting message shortly before its precipitous flight, wanted to keep the station on the air to cover its departure; perhaps it was due to the presence of fifth column activity within the station; or it may have been simply that no adequate demolition plan existed.

The North Koreans brought with them men from their own radio system for the top personnel jobs of Radio Seoul (the chief engineer had been trained in Moscow). Every effort, however, was made to keep the station's lower personnel, particularly the technicians, in their jobs. The engineers, the writers, the announcers, were assured that they had nothing to fear if they would cooperate. Thus, the occupation government controlled the program content but the work of putting it on the air was carried on by the usual South Korean personnel.

All seven newspapers in Seoul were suspended by the occupation authorities. In their place, they reinstated the *People's Daily News* and the *Liberation Daily News,* two papers previously suspended by the R.O.K. government because of their Communistic lines. It appears they reinstated also the South Korean Communist editors of the earlier publications. The papers were nationalized. They were printed in Seoul's largest newspaper offices which had been confiscated for the purpose. All news services except TASS were also forbidden. In addition to TASS, most of the news that was to be printed came from the many releases and articles sent to the newspaper offices by the Public Information Office. Here, too, we see the common pattern in operation: continue to use the same technical personnel (printers, circulation men, etc.), but put the control of the policy line and content into the hands of the Party and the government (Communist editors, TASS, the Public Information Office).

For several weeks these newspapers were distributed gratis, apparently in the ratio of one paper to every six or eight homes. Each family which received a copy was asked to read the paper, then hand it to a neighbor. Then, after several weeks a charge was made for the papers, although apparently some free circulation did continue. After the occupation had ended, it was impossible to obtain accurate information on circulation trends and patterns.

Control of the motion pictures shown in Seoul theatres was maintained through the Cultural Bureau of the Home Ministry. United States and British films were excluded. It was estimated that three out of every five films shown were of Russian origin. A few films from China or other "non-capitalist" countries were also shown. Pictures were chosen for their ideological and propagandistic content, and there appears to have been a considerable repetition of films shown.

During the first few weeks of occupation, admission to the theatres was free, which contributed greatly to the popularity of the occupation government and kept attendance high. Then, so it is said, one night during the performance the theatre doors were locked and all able-bodied men of military age in the audience were seized and conscripted into the army. As a result attendance thereafter fell to a small percentage of its former size. This story is encountered so often there seems little reason to doubt it.

The same news and many of the same articles would appear in both newspapers, and the newspapers would often be read over the radio. The same political articles would be sent by the Public Information Office to both papers and radio, and news for all the media was filtered through TASS. Reports all agree that there was a great sameness of content in all mass communications during the occupation period regardless of media. The movies, with their strong ideological content, repeated the same line, with many of the same illustrations, that was given in the newspapers and on the radio.

There is also general agreement that in the newspapers, radio, movies, there was a high percentage of formalized political content—political speeches and discussions, letters and messages to and from leading Communists, explanation of doctrinary points. This obviously was at the cost of entertainment on the radio and of social news in the papers. "Radio Seoul," said one resident, "was just talk, talk, talk." "There was no charm in press and radio," said another. "The radio was just mechanical propaganda," said a writer. "Of course the Communists didn't have a privately owned press," a publisher remarked wryly, "they only had to consider what went in, not how nor what the people thought of it."

The Communists, of course, depended on their monopoly to remove their need of competing for an audience. They did not have to worry if their newspapers and radio programs were a little on the dull and preachy side. They conceived the press and radio, and especially the former, as a kind of textbook, and used them as such. At the culture hours, the newspaper was read to the meeting. "We had to pass on to others the exact content of the speeches given by leaders without adding a single word of our own," explained one Seoul resident.

Never forgetting their ultimate purpose, the Communists made several important changes in media form and content. To reach the larger audience which was more familiar with Korean phonetic characters than with the more commonly printed Chinese ideographs, use of the Korean characters was emphasized. There is also testimony that they rearranged the contents of the papers to make them easier for unlearned readers to use. On Radio Seoul they frequently reserved spots for laborers and farmers to be interviewed and to speak their political thoughts.

Such changes as these, of course, were made as a gesture to their audience. Changes were also made in the interest of building up the Party. They used the front page of the newspaper for speeches by Russian Communist leaders or for messages to and from Kim Il Sung. On the radio, they programmed a generous amount of military music, and a great many political talks. These talks were "sometimes one and a half hours," one respondent said, and were "often read mechanically, without pause, from the newspaper." They carried an uncommon amount of abuse for the United States and the United Nations, but only favorable news when it concerned the Communists.

During the ninety days of occupation, it appears the Communists did not accomplish too much through the radio and other mass media. There are indications that, if there had been time to develop their program further, public reaction might have been more responsive. Another factor operated against immediate Communist success. Their audience was one which had been accustomed to a relatively free press and it was not wholly isolated from an entertaining radio. Many complained that the news was the same in all media. Some said they became surfeited with the mutual admiration of the top Communists. One person interviewed, however, said, "The information we got through the press and radio was just like the contents of a textbook on Communism." Perhaps he had come nearer the Communists' purpose than he realized.

An interesting footnote to Communist handling of newspaper production was the fact that there were apparently very few misprints and typographical errors. Whenever an editor or proofreader made a misprint in the paper, a Seoul publisher explained, he was required to make a public "self-criticism." After a few such "self-criticisms," punishment was doubtless more direct.

Like the radio and newspapers, the Public Information Office was headed by North Korean imported personnel, and the South Korean under-personnel were "encouraged" to stay on, particularly the artists who drew posters and placards. "If you cooperate, you have nothing to fear. If you do not cooperate, you will be shot. From this day, you will be watched."

Artists were particularly encouraged, for the occupation government made widespread use of pictorial communications. In general, the pictorial quality was excellent. Many of the posters, of course, were imported, some even from Russia. Many of these imports bore pictures of Kim Il Sung, Stalin, or Lenin, and all of them followed the simple propaganda line previously laid down. They were often in bright colors and some were extremely well printed. A favorite technique seems to have been a "salvo of posters" at an important point. Tons of posters and leaflets came in with the occupation troops, but despite this ready supply the occupation authorities preferred to have their first posters hand-lettered in Seoul. These welcomed the People's army, and were painted in fairly crude fashion to give the impression of a spontaneous outburst of enthusiasm.

Leaflets were given out in great profusion at meetings, at factories, and business places, and sometimes on a house-to-house basis. Most of these were basic explanations of defenses of Communism and the People's government. There was also a considerable supply of Russian magazines, many of them beautifully printed and composed chiefly of pictures. The Communists made a special effort to reinforce the propaganda of the formal media of communication through personal contacts. The first wave of occupation soldiers had apparently had special training in this aspect of propaganda. A Seoul businessman described their conduct thus: "At the earliest stage of their occupation, every soldier behaved himself like a political officer, preaching Communism outside and inside his barracks at off times and being very friendly toward the people. They tried to leave the unpleasant duties of arrest and search to their agents." This careful friendliness and the studied use of every contact with the South Korean people to advance the cause of Communism, a fact widely reported, is evidence of the fine attention to propaganda detail which characterizes the sovietized state.

Non-military persons were also given assignments in face-to-face propaganda. In every principal Communist organization a certain number of members were assigned, probably on a rotation basis, to make personal visits to citizens in the interests of building up the Party. Members of the Youth Alliance, for example, were assigned to visit parents at home to persuade them to return their children to school.

An interesting footnote to this technique of "personalized" propaganda is added by a lieutenant of the psychological warfare section of the North Korean 15th Division, captured in September 1950. After describing his apparently well-staffed divisional organization, he went on to report that his section often had leaflets, written by the mothers and fathers of R.O.K. prisoners, for distribution to their friends and neighbors urging surrender and the ultimate unification of Korea. At times, he said, it was also the custom to release prisoners, suitably indoctrinated, to return to their own lines and gather information or persuade other troops to cease fighting.

There were also full-time agitators who were, in effect, official rumor-mongers. Some of these were avowed representatives, some were merely grey propaganda vehicles.

It was from one of these, on September 25, 1950, that a doctor's wife learned that the Inchon invaders had been "driven back into the sea and the invasion annihilated." Just how important these agitators were in the scheme of sovietization is impossible to tell from the evidence at hand in Seoul. Nor is it possible to say whether they had any responsibilities for surveillance as well as propaganda. The fact remains that there were a number of such agitators, and they seem to have been active.

Meetings, however, were the most important devices for word-of-mouth sovietization, as it revealed itself in Korea in the summer of 1950. Almost every personal account of the occupation emphasizes the great number of meetings. "We were forced to attend meetings every morning at seven," reported a beer wholesaler. "If we were absent we were supposed to receive 'training.' Sometimes we had to attend meetings four or five times a day."

Not only were these meetings frequent, they were also of many kinds; alliance meetings, community or industry meetings, "culture hours," criticism and reflection meetings, rallies, parades and spectacles.

The chief purpose of alliance meetings (the Women's Alliance and the Youth Alliance), usually held daily or every few days by the Communist Party, was to receive orders and assign duties. Community or industry meetings, held at irregular intervals, were intended to make converts and confirm believers.

"Culture hours" were usually held daily in professional associations, schools, and places of business. A Seoul professional man reported that at this type of meeting "the people in attendance read aloud an article (on Communism) or a speech (by one of the chief Communists) in a newspaper, pamphlet, or book, and discussed it with each other. Or they reported on some Communist literature they had read outside the meeting. Attendance was compulsory. If absent, a person was considered to be reactionary." In the criticism and reflection meetings, citizens were supposed to admit and ask pardon for their defections, or to meditate on their defections.

Rallies, parades and spectacles were huge meetings conducted in the best totalitarian tradition to celebrate some major event. Such a gala meeting, with speeches, a symphony orchestra, huge choruses, and dancers under the direction of Korea's greatest musical conductor, had been planned for Seoul at the end of September.

The Communists attached great importance in their scheme of things to the schools, and the occupation government began at once to remake the schools of Seoul to serve its own ends. The fact that their efforts did not meet with great success may be attributed partly to shortness of the time, partly to disturbing conditions such as air raids, and partly to administrative failure.

The Minister of Education brought in by the Communists was a former principal of a girls' high school in Seoul who had gone to North Korea several years before. He told the teachers to come back, that they had nothing to fear if they would cooperate. The same message went to the employees of the Ministry of Education. The top men and most of the extreme anti-Communists went into hiding or escaped to the south. Those who did return were put into courses designed to re-educate them in the principles of the new government. The forty members of the Ministry who returned, however, were given severe manual labor as a part of their "course." This, they were told, was punishment for their cooperation with the R.O.K. government. University professors in social science fields were put through courses lasting two to three weeks which largely consisted of lectures by students from the Kim Il Sung University of Pyongyang. These courses were described as dull and poorly planned. Lectures were delivered mechanically and from memory. When a lecture was over, there might be hours of waiting, for attendance was compulsory between 8 A.M. and 5 P.M. The exact nature of the course given teachers in the lower and middle schools is not clearly known, but like all courses they included self-criticism, sometimes written, sometimes spoken.

A minor staff member of the University of Seoul told this story of his experiences:

> I was working as a research assistant at the university. On June 27 at seven in the evening I heard that the R.O.K. army would destroy the Han River bridge, but I didn't think that Seoul would be captured soon. At ten, when I heard artillery in the distance, I consulted with one of my housemates about what to do. He was very calm. (He later turned out to be a member of the South Korean Labor [Communist] Party.)
>
> No sleep that night. The next day Seoul was captured. The following three days I stayed at home, then on the fourth day I went back to my college. It was being used partly for Red soldiers. Some of the college equipment had been destroyed by Red students. Many of the Red students and professors formed the so-called Self-Governing Committee of the college. I found out that the heads of the chemistry and physics departments had turned out to be Communists.

I was asked to submit my personal history to the Self-Governing Committee, but never did. Later, after the recapture of Seoul, all of the personal histories submitted to the Self-Governing Committee by professors and assistants were found, and it was quite convenient for the college authorities to identify the Red elements within the college.

Toward the end of July, I visited the college out of curiosity. (All this time I had been keeping out of the Communists' way.) All the former professors were busy transferring their authority to the Self-Governing Committee. I was ordered to go to a certain place in the city to get my Communist re-education. I went there for three days, and then I stayed home.

My worry was how to avoid being recruited as a soldier for the People's army. From the beginning of August to the end of the occupation I kept myself hidden under the roof of the house.

The primary schools in Seoul were renamed People's Schools. All statues and pictures of South Korean dignitaries were removed, and pictures of Stalin and Kim Il Sung put in their places. It was announced that Russian would be substituted for English as a foreign language in the curriculum, and that, as in North Korea, the Korean phonetic alphabet would be taught. With an occupation that lasted only ninety days and with a shortage of teachers, textbooks, and students, there was little opportunity to make many changes in curriculum or to impose the blueprint already created in the North Korean system.

Many teachers had fled, were discharged, or had stopped teaching. The turnover of teachers in many schools was almost complete. Almost all those who represented advanced educational thought in Korea, especially those trained in the United States or by the U. S. Educational Mission, were replaced. Many of the new teachers, though safe politically, were not well trained educationally. It was possible, for example, for a primary school graduate to teach primary school with no further professional training (but not without further training in Communist indoctrination). There was little to do in class, however, for new textbooks were apparently not available in sufficient quantities.

In some schools, attendance at summer's end was less than twenty per cent of what it had been in June. Students stayed away because: (1) schools were used as places to draft for the army; (2) many school buildings were used as barracks; (3) air raids were frequent and provided a good excuse to keep children at home; and (4) some parents felt (and many students agreed) that the children were not learning much. "I didn't send our children," a typical Seoul mother reported, "because they only taught children songs, and we were afraid of air raids." The great emphasis on song lessons and the classroom time spent on "culture" were two characteristics of the school curriculum in Seoul during the summer of 1950 which were mentioned in almost every interview with parents or students. For two or more hours at a time, the children were taught Communist songs. "Culture" was taught from a textbook to which only the teacher had access and from which students were required to learn and repeat by rote. By common report, no one found it inspiring.

In spite of lack of time and unfavorable conditions, however, many of the characteristics of the North Korean educational system began to emerge—plans for building more schools, remaking the primary school as a real people's school to attack illiteracy and ignorance on the broadest basis, use of the Korean alphabet, writing Communistic history and dialectical materialism into all history and social studies, and organization of a strong Youth Alliance in all schools. It is reasonable to think that, given more time, the pattern would have emerged completely. It is also reasonable to think that the Communists would have solved the teacher problem, at least to their own satisfaction, for education is such a strong part of sovietization that failure such as the fall in enrollment in Seoul would not have been tolerated for very long.

Each of the three central organizations of the Soviet state in Seoul—the Communist Party (or Korean Labor Party, as it was called), the Women's Alliance, and the Youth Alliance—was a powerful agent of ideological propaganda. Together they spoke for the Party to most of the citizens of Seoul.

The Women's Alliance held a weekly propaganda lecture and discussion. The continuing subject was that women should have equality with men—that the R.O.K. government had subjugated and restrained women, and how, under the People's Republic, the women had their first opportunity to break the traditional patterns of male authority. The leader of this organization came from North Korea. There was a sub-leader for every village and for every small section of Seoul. Each leader was responsible for every house in her district. Her duties were to distribute pamphlets, make speeches, and go from door to door to tell people about the program. The association built up slowly. After some weeks the leaders began to check attendance. Gradually attendance became compulsory. Absence from association meetings was *prima facie* evidence that the absentee was against the government. "Attendance" must be distinguished from "joining"; an invitation to join the association was an honor and a woman who refused such an invitation was in danger of "disappearing."

The democratic Youth Alliance functioned more or less as a secret organization. It was organized through the schools with the familiar care and thoroughness. It had a secret sign and password. A small secret group of members were guardians of the association's policy. Each day they issued orders to the other members, assigning them such duties as writing signs or visiting certain houses. The ultimate source of these orders was always kept veiled. Even the transmission process was kept hidden, for a member knew only from whom the order was received and to whom, in turn, the order was to be given. This was the organization that, when attendance declined, was ordered to visit all the houses in town in an attempt to persuade parents to send their children to school.

It must not be forgotten that the most powerful of all the organizations nurtured by the occupation was the Communist Party itself. The organization of the Party, with its secret inner circle and direct authority, its almost military control, its scrupulous attention to detail, in every way served as a pattern to be applied to the supplementary organizations (such as the Women's Alliance and the Youth Alliance) it controlled.

The Communists took over all the powerful occupational organizations that were in existence when they came, including the Labor Union (composed of about thirteen hundred local unions) and the chief professional and business associations. Government officials made sure that trusted Communists were in positions of high authority, and as far as possible put Communist representatives in strategic spots throughout local units to lead and spy. In each organization they instituted cultural hours, lectures, special meetings, and other devices of political re-education. Even the doctors, it will be recalled, were obliged to meet at least one hour every day to read the newspaper to each other and discuss "assigned readings" in Communism. Reading material was placed in most of the associations' headquarters, and in every district and village a "room of democratic propaganda" was established where newspapers, books, posters, and pictures would be found. Lecturers, who were provided for cultural meetings, were often bright young men from Kim Il Sung University who gave memorized and more or less mechanical renderings of dull political discussions. The Communists made sure that their organization members were bombarded with politically safe material.

In order to train Party leaders, propaganda specialists, cultural officers for the army, and others who would most represent the aims and beliefs of the state through propaganda, the Soviet system included an elaborate group of training schools. Such a system had been well developed also in North Korea, and during the brief occupation period elements of it were reproduced in Seoul. Curricula of a few northern schools give some evidence of the general character of the system. For example, the Central Political School at Pyongyang to which many potential Party leaders from South Korea were sent was a ten-month course with forty-six class hours a week. It included the following subjects: Russian Language, History of the

Communist Party, Politics, History of Korea, World Political Geography, Military Tactics, and Physical Training.

A similar school to train labor leaders offered a four-month course (as well as special short courses) in the following subjects: Korean Labor History, World Labor Organization History, World Economic Development, Current News, and International Relations in Modern History.

Schools set up to train cultural officers for the Communist armies typically included: Korean History, Politics, World Political Geography, Mathematics, and Russian Language.

Even professional schools were filled with indoctrination courses. Engineering, legal, and all technical students at Pyongyang were required to attend one and one-half hours of "cultural" classes a day. At Haeju Normal College the historical section made sure that teachers took courses in Marxism and Leninism, European History, Korean History, Russian Language, Russian Teaching Methods, and First Aid.

Music, the theatre, parades, and huge spectacles all had an important part to play in the Communist scheme of things. Occupation leaders made frequent use of ideological songs (North Korean, Russian, International Communist) at their meetings, in the schools, in the streets. They also made frequent use of short plays to illustrate some point in their propaganda line. These dramas were presented by visiting North Korean actors, or by casts recruited from the local Communist Party or the schools. Parades were arranged as often as possible, in which various associations and North Korean troops took a prominent part. One of the most ironic chapters in the occupation history concerned one of the largest parades in the history of Seoul, minutely organized by the Communists and featuring all the Communist organizations and many colorful groups and exhibits. It was held on the day after the Inchon landing "to celebrate the fact that the invaders had been pushed back into the sea!"

For artists, as for technicians, the Communist occupation government showed respect. Many times in the years between 1947 and 1950, the North Korean government invited South Korean musicians and writers to come to the North. Some of these they offered to send to Moscow for more training.

After the invasion they took further steps to make friends of this group. They appeared to be quite willing to forgive artists any past cooperation with the R.O.K. government, were even willing to forgive active and past opposition to the Communists, and offered those who would agree to cooperate "another chance." The conductor of the Seoul Philharmonic, for example, an internationally known musician who had studied and conducted in the United States, had spurned previous invitations and urgings from the Communists, but he was excused for his past deviations on his promise to conduct for the new government. He was even put into North Korean uniform and named director of the Red Army chorus. A similar pattern was apparently followed in many other such cases, although there were artists who complained they had been assigned to paint only pictures of Stalin and Kim Il Sung.

Similar overtures, it appears, were also made in the

field of sports. The international reputation of some athletes made them good propaganda vehicles for an international audience. Just before the invasion Sohn Ki-Jung and his fellow marathon runners returned to Seoul after their victory in Boston. When arrested, they were commanded to broadcast political propaganda to foreign nations. They were able to escape, however, and went underground for the duration of the occupation.

Some of these writers and technicians who accepted the Communist proviso of cooperation, found themselves not very happy in their choice. One South Korean writer in Seoul testified thus:

> I have written anti-Communist novels, so I feared I might be arrested by the Reds. Right after their entry into Seoul, many leftist writers advised me to join the Union of Writers, otherwise I might be considered a dangerous element. Three weeks later I joined the group. Once they told me to be a spy among rightist writers, but I refused and hid myself. Then, upon the advice of the Union of Writers, to save my life I applied for the position of propagandist. I was supposed to be re-educated for this job in North Korea, but when I was sent to North Korea instead of being re-educated I was forced to become a laborer in a coal mine near Kae-Chun. With the help of a non-Communist North Korean soldier I met there, I managed to run away from the coal mine. I did not have any identification card with me, and it was lucky I did not meet any Communist officials or I would have been shot.

When the Reds packed up and left Seoul they took with them all the distinguished musicians and writers they could round up, in addition to the contents of numerous museums and the books from many of the libraries in the city.

Despite all the skill and effort expended on it, the monopoly of communication was not completely airtight. The experience of an electrician employed by the Ministry of Communications in Seoul is a case in point:

> For a month or so after the occupation, I did my work quietly, talked to nobody, and hurried home to spend the night in fear the Communists would come for me. They told us they wouldn't bother us if we cooperated, but I didn't believe them. However, because I wasn't very important or perhaps because they felt they needed communication technicians too much to bother me, they left me alone.
>
> Gradually I began to feel easier and to look around me to see what I could do. Several of us, old friends, began to meet together. At first we just sat and had a drink. Everybody was afraid to talk, because everybody thought everyone else might be a spy. But at last someone dared whisper what we all were thinking. "What can we do?" we asked each other.
>
> We began to meet together every third night, always at a different house. We would take a little radio receiver and go down under the floor and wrap the receiver and ourselves in quilts and listen to the news, usually from Japan, sometimes from San Francisco. It was stifling in those bed clothes, but they prevented the radio from being heard. After listening, each of us would go and tell the news to people around his home. In this way we managed to get the true news into almost every part of Seoul.
>
> When we got a leaflet from the U.N. forces we would memorize the contents and pass the information along in the same way.

> We also began to think what we could do to sabotage communications without being caught. We decided to make some bad splices, and to find out how to blow a transformer easily so when it would help most we could do it.
>
> I was elected to the Self-Governing Committee, but the Communists on the committee were so overbearing toward us that it was a comfort in meetings to think about how we were striking a few blows behind their backs. And then the Communists accused me of making bad splices and I had to hide, but before I could do anything underground the U.S. troops came in.

The most effective weapon against the Communist monopoly of information in Seoul was the radio receiver. Every Seoul resident interviewed confirmed this. Even after such listening became illegal and highly dangerous "I ventured to listen anyway in order to get some news." "While my husband listened indoors in the blackout to the Japanese news broadcast or the Voice of America, I stood post outside." Radio sets were concealed in bedding, under mats, in walls. They were used for only a few minutes at a time, then the news was passed by word of mouth between trusted friends. In Seoul, every radio set was a pipe line to the families of all the friends of the owner. In villages, the market became a center of United Nations news. The U.N. leaflets which reached the residents of Seoul were another though lesser danger to the Communist monopoly.

The Communists, however, did not underestimate the effect of either radio or leaflets, but made it as difficult as possible for either of these media to break through. They were willing to confiscate radios, even at the sacrifice of audiences for their own broadcasts and to make it a serious offense to be caught either listening to the U.N. broadcast or picking up a U.N. leaflet. Even so, people took the risk.

SELF-CRITICISM

"Self-criticism," or "confession" was a device of thought control used for both diagnosis and therapy. In a written or oral statement the maker admitted his previous defections from the ideology and practices of Communism and the People's Republic, and expressed his contrition.

Akin to the self-criticism and sometimes merging into it was the "personal history," or biography, in which a person recorded what one Seoul citizen described as his past "from the age of eight to the present," his home affairs, occupation, relations with the political party, and whether or not he had ever been imprisoned for Red (or anti-Red) action. In contrast to self-criticism, personal history was used primarily as a fact-gathering device.

In the training schools set up for persons such as teachers, communications executives, etc., who would have considerable influence over the thinking of their countrymen, the writing of self-criticisms was almost a daily exercise. In addition, oral confessions sometimes had to be made to a representative of the Communist Party. In shorter courses consisting mostly of lectures, for example the one-week indoctrination course for technicians, self-criticism seems to have been used as a final examination by which the Communists could discover whether or not their doctrine had been accepted and whether or not the person would be a trustworthy cooperator.

But self-criticism was not restricted to specialized training courses for key personnel. About July 11, an announcement was made that all citizens should go to their nearest police station by July 15 and "confess." How many did go is not accurately known but they numbered in the tens of thousands.

Compliance with an order for self-criticism also frequently involved all the members of specific groups. For example, one engineer said that after his association had debated the order, it was decided that all of them would confess. The same story was told about associations of doctors and lawyers. On an individual basis, these men may have been reluctant to obey the order, but they drew strength from the group decision.

So far as is known, written copies of these self-criticisms are not available, although it is known that a number of personal histories were found when at least one Seoul educational institution was repossessed from the invader (they provided helpful reading later for the administrators who were trying to get rid of Communist elements within the faculty). It is likely, however, that many self-criticisms are preserved in Communist dossiers, marked for later action.

The pressure to "confess" was considerable. In the training courses and re-education programs, of course, it was compulsory. In the meetings of community associations, the Women's Alliance and the Youth Alliance, it was common for one member to charge another with misdeeds, and then for the accused to have to mount the platform and make an oral self-criticism. Among the general public, the pressure of opinion and the threat of official harm both operated to encourage confession. Again and again, stories were told in Seoul of how friends would come to a man and suggest he submit a personal criticism to satisfy the Party and mollify his critics. The usual reaction to such a suggestion either avoided or, more often, postponed action. "I explained that I was without distinction, therefore a personal criticism from me would be valueless," or "I explained that I had always been a non-political person," represent typical answers. If the pressure became too strong, and the resistance to confession did not relax, the only thing left to do was to go into hiding. For some lucky people, the end of the occupation came before pressure became so great as to force this action.

On the surface, such a device would seem likely to encourage lying and fantasy; and many people crossed their fingers and did just that, because to satisfy the demand for confession was the only way to get along with the new government. "I confessed," said one Seoul businessman, "but I did not write the true fact." Nevertheless, there is a considerable body of testimony that the device worked exactly as the Communists wanted it to work. It served first of all to point out the more hardened opponents of Communism whose scruples would not let them confess; such people could then be earmarked as poor material for conversion and cooperation. Secondly, it served to focus the attention of the people on the values and ideology of Communism; if they did not know the law, they would not know what wrong to confess to. Finally, self-confession seemed to have a considerable suggestive power. It looked like a highly plausible and reasonable emotional outlet, and one that had the advantage of mass reinforcement. All over the city, thousands of persons were confessing to the same errors, the tide carrying them on like a religious revival. There is reason to think that persons who at first approached self-criticism with tongue in cheek soon began to believe their own confessions which, in turn, inspired a greater willingness on their part to cooperate with the new regime.

Although as an instrument of thought control and conversion it may be assumed that self-criticism was a success, as a guide to administrative action, the degree of success is less clear. Again, the time element may have been responsible. An emotional effect takes much less time to achieve than calculated administrative action. The Communists appeared, however, to think that confessions gave them a good indication of who would be poor risks as cooperators, and it was apparently on this basis that they dismissed a number of teachers at the end of their training course. On the same basis they got rid of many already in teaching jobs and broke up ideological groups. Just what use was made of the confessions turned in by the general public at the police stations is not known.

When a Communist propaganda program has been operative for five years in a satellite state, as in North Korea, it is possible to begin to measure its effectiveness. A three-month operation, as in Seoul during the summer of 1950, cannot, of course, provide an adequate set of benchmarks. Yet even in this short period of occupation, certain aspects of success in their program stand out. The Communists were remarkably successful in the concentration of their efforts on a simple and well-conceived propaganda line and in reinforcing this line with every channel of communication from the largest of the mass media to the most intimate kind of face-to-face indoctrination. All evidence is to the effect that the propaganda *did* reach the people, and that they were caught up in the organization activities, cultural hours, and other semi-active parts of the indoctrination program. Communist efforts in these respects were at least partially successful, but the leaks in their dike (U.N. radio and U.N. leaflets) were highly important.

Not only did the Communists succeed in reaching the people, they succeeded also in getting people to work actively in the re-education program, and in monopolizing all but a tiny fraction of the people's communication time. It is hard to tell just how convincing they were, but certain bits of indirect evidence indicate that the propaganda program was beginning to pay dividends, in spite of the fact that they had to work amidst the distractions of war and with a population to whom the memory of a free press and an entertaining radio was still fresh. "As we heard the same thing many times," a Seoul doctor commented, "we could not help but memorize it, though we felt tired." "As they repeated the same lecture with the same words, I began to find myself listening to them," was the report of a school boy. Nor did the friendly attitude of those personal propaganda representatives, the first North Korean People's army garrison (which may have come in large part from the Korean members of the Chinese Communist forces Eighth Route army) go unappreciated. The admiration of the populace was frequently expressed for the efficiency, the vigor, the discipline of the Communist state they saw displayed. That three months of sovietizing propaganda in Seoul did make considerable progress, from the Communist point of view, is certain.

Yoon-Sook Mo

Pursued by the Secret Police

Yoon-Sook Mo, "one of the most beautiful women in Korea," was the woman the Communists were trying to kill when Mrs. Underwood, wife of an American missionary, was assassinated.

At noon on June 25 the Pyongyang radio announced, "Because the so-called National army of southern Korea started an invasion of northern Korea, we, who have been trying to unify our country through peaceful means, unwillingly have in retaliation ordered a general attack."

I turned the dial to the Seoul station and heard that the puppet army had at daybreak crossed the 38th parallel.

On the 27th the refugees began coming into Seoul. Waves of people rushed through the streets with loads on their heads, in their hands, on their backs. Over the radio came the admonition not to be troubled, to refrain from hasty action and thoughtless movement. The voice assured us that tomorrow morning there would be planes from General MacArthur's forces, and within a few days ground forces to cooperate in the defense of Seoul. But it was already too late to halt the panic. People rushed this way and that, seeking refuge wherever possible, and the streets were congested with refugees.

In order to see more of what was taking place, I got in a jeep and drove outside the city proper. On the highways I saw truckloads of National soldiers returning to the city, but thought that they were merely being relieved by other soldiers. I believed that by the next day the fighting would be far away from Seoul. Even when a bullet whizzed past my ear, my faith in the National army was strong and unshaken.

I returned to the city and, not taking time to eat supper, rushed to the radio station for my broadcast. From the studio window I saw that the commotion in the streets had increased. I finished my broadcast and hurried home by jeep.

The windows and floors soon began to shake with the thunderings of the cannonade. I was frantic for news and tried to telephone, but the line was cut off. Although my driver and police guard were with me, an uncontrollable sense of emptiness overwhelmed me. The noise of the guns was terrifying and, thinking that we would be safer in the basement, we went there and spent the rest of the night. The noise from outside did not abate, but I tried to comfort myself with the belief that all the racket was being made by our National army.

At sunrise, thinking that the enemy had been repelled from the city, I opened the basement door and cautiously looked out. But when I stepped out on the street I discovered that I had made a grave error. All my hopes of the night before vanished when I saw on the side of the street terrifying displays of Soviet-made tanks and puppet soldiery. I could not believe that Seoul had gone into the hands of the puppets. But the populace had vanished and the streets were filled with trucks of the puppets and noisy with the sound of soldiers' footsteps and reports of their burp guns. Rather than by fear, I was pressed down by a heavy sensation of suffocation as I went back indoors.

My driver and police guard urged me to gather my senses and escape as quickly as possible. Just at that moment, I heard the rough voices of puppet soldiers from outside the gate and like lightning a bullet pierced the door of the room and flew in. I do not know where the strength came from, but as if by a reflex I sprang up and ran out the back gate and into the alley, with a resounding "Mansei" echoing behind me.

Climbing the Namsan [South Mountain], I came to a church and hid in the basement. Then, toward sundown, I put a towel around my head and walked toward Sinchon. My plan was to see President Helen Kim of the Ewha University and perhaps escape together. In the middle of a wide thoroughfare I stopped in horror when I saw lined up at the darkening street corner more than a hundred captured National soldiers being cruelly shot down with burp guns. My breast almost burst with anger and pain. Having no way to save the falling men, I offered my prayer for their blessings in the other world. Then, knowing that if I were discovered I would meet the same fate, I hurried on.

I do not know how I reached the hill back of the President's residence, but when I got there the puppet soldiers had already surrounded the house and I could not get past them to enter. The sun was setting and I hoped that darkness would hasten and enshroud me, for now I had nowhere to go.

Suddenly I thought of going out to the river at Mapo and started in that direction. I felt my way in the deepening darkness and reached the bank with the ceaseless reports of the guns tearing at my ears. The loneliness of no one to lean on brought hot tears to my eyes. It seemed to me that I must either die or be captured, and I resolved to die. As I stood on the edge of the river a young man came out from nowhere and restrained me. I was so startled that I stepped back a little. For half an hour he tried to convince me of the futility of suicide and urged me to wait a few days, for the American army would surely recapture Seoul. As I became certain that he was not a Communist but a friend, my paralyzed mind was somewhat restored. With no further hesitation I went with him to his house and hid in a storage space. I also ate some rice.

News came that American planes were flying over Seoul. I believed that the defeated National army would be reorganized and, in cooperation with the American planes, would recapture Seoul in a few days. Instead, a report came that the puppets had taken Suwon.

After I had been in the young man's house for three days, he coolly told me that he could not hide me any longer. Unable to offer any resistance, I thanked him for helping me and, that night, took to the nearest hillside. I went over two hills and came to an unoccupied thatched cottage. The next day I bought some potatoes with the money I still had with me. In the daytime I hid under a rock, and at night I looked up at the Silver Stream [the Milky Way].

Among the refugees coming over the hills in the night were people who related the atrocities perpetrated in Seoul, so even in this deep valley I heard the sad news.

Though I had hoped to hold out here as long as life lasted, it was not to be. After a few days I heard through refugees that the Bureau of Internal Affairs [Police Office] had sent out its men to search for me in this area.

I gathered my confused thoughts together to try to think out a way of escape. Before me lay a wide river, blocking any thought of going south. It seemed that the best plan was to go in the opposite direction, piercing through the city and beyond the East Gate. To try to break through the city when the Communists were searching for me was more than a dangerous risk, but I decided to take the chance.

On July 15 I started out, dizzy and shaking from having been famished for many days. I changed my hair to the old style, put on an old skirt, and started out with bare feet, looking as much like a country woman as possible.

My feet began to trouble me when I was barely over the pass. When the pain became too great I put on shoes [slipper-like and made of rubber], but they would not stay on because of the blood oozing from my feet. I plucked a handful of tall grass and wrapped them, and the warm fragrance was refreshing to my empty stomach.

As I stepped out into the avenue leading to the heart of the city, I saw soldiers of the puppet army examining passersby. There were four soldiers altogether, threatening people in rough language and at times striking them with the butts of their guns. Some passersby knelt down, trembling. Even though I had foreseen this, when I came to it my limbs shook like aspen leaves and I felt I would fall.

One of the soldiers was demanding loudly, "Have you not seen a woman named Yoon-Sook Mo in this mountain? We know that she is hiding in this mountain; if you don't tell the truth, you'll be taken for a reactionary and shot." The questioner struck the man's shoulder with the butt of a gun.

"Even if I were put to death, I wouldn't know. I've not seen her." It was the voice of an old man who looked like a merchant.

The soldiers' speech betrayed their Hamkyang origin, and I made up my mind to use after these long years my home country brogue of Hamkyang when my turn came.

I waited, with the rubber shoes in my hands and on my head a bag of potatoes hanging almost over my eyes.

"Where to going?" was the first brusque question.

"Going to sell potatoes," I simulated an ignorant woman.

"Auntie from Hamkyang Doo?" the soldier asked, pretending to be glad.

"How not? From my Hamhung about ten years."

"So you've not heard that a woman named Yoon-Sook Mo is in hiding over this mountain?" he asked in a loud voice. Like lightning the trembling hit my arms and legs.

"How could I know such woman? Under heaven I hear such a name for the first time. Hurry and let me go. You ask strange things to an ignorant woman who does not even know a 'k' " [first letter in the Korean alphabet].

They were talking in whispers and then one of them took a photograph from his pocket and looked at it. My limbs were trembling again, and there was "double clubbing" in my breast [double clubbing is a process by which Korean women smooth and gloss cloth]. No matter how well one may be disguised, once comparison is made with a photograph, that is the end. If I were caught now, atrocious torture was certain. But luckily the get-up in the photograph and my present appearance and behavior seemed too dissimilar to them. The man looked me up and down and then showed me the photograph, saying, "You can go, but when you see a woman like that, you will have to report to Internal Affairs Station." At a glance I found that it was a small photograph of me in some fineries, taken in Paris two years earlier.

"Of course I'll report. Let me look once again." I pretended to look once more and then started off.

Perspiration streamed down my back, my eyes burned

as if on fire. I wanted to cry but, fearing those behind, swallowed my tears and walked on. I was oppressed by a feeling that those who accosted me were coming to overtake me.

When I reached the height of Ahyon the number of passersby increased and it made me jittery again. But I took courage and walked on to the streets where the so-called war news, the pictures of Kim Il Sung and of Stalin, and red flags were in abundant evidence.

I reached the slum district under Raksan [Mountain] as the nine o'clock curfew hour approached, and I knew I had to get off the streets. I stopped at a thatched house and gave a sum of what remained of my money for a bowl of barley gruel. Shaken by fear, fatigue and hunger, I ate the gruel with a relish that can be appreciated only by those who have had a similar experience.

The atmosphere of the house was so benevolent that I asked if I might stay there for a few days. There were twelve in the family and they were so poor that sometimes they had only one meal of barley gruel a day. They were Catholics and the man was a class leader in the neighborhood organization. For one month I hid in the storage space in the wall, in the kitchen, and in the basement.

Surprisingly they had a radio set and from time to time I heard the propaganda news of the puppets. One night a member of the National Assembly made a broadcast supposedly in support of the puppet regime. The utter hopelessness in his voice was so painful that I could not hear the speech through. Rather than meet the same fate myself, I again determined to take my life with my own hands. I had some opium with me for such an emergency and I resolved to use it. I could no longer endure this life without some hope to hold onto. The occasional radio news always told of the puppet victory. Our National army, for which we waited, did not come. Dogged anguish and hunger taxed me to the limit. This was truly a life in hell.

I went out to the yard and stood on the soy sauce platform [a platform where many jars of two- to five-barrel capacity are kept the year round for sunning and aging purposes]. As a last joy I drank in the clear atmosphere and looked up in the sky. I turned my back on the North Star and faced the southern horizon. Then I pushed myself between the big jars and while aimless tears streamed down my face I swallowed three opium pills.

But the opium only drugged me into a deep sleep, and after two days I was awake again, tortured by severe hunger and thirst. The master of the house was urging me in a tone of great fright to leave. The police had made a house-to-house search carrying my photograph with them, and I had escaped detection only because I was in a coma. Since this whole family was about to suffer because of me, there was nothing to do but leave.

At dawn I left the house and started walking toward the mountain peak. It was very foggy that morning and I felt that no one could see me.

As I passed a group of women selling unleavened rice bread I felt excruciating pain inside me. I stopped and like a madwoman looked down on the steaming bread, gulping saliva. I did not have a cent. Each of the competitors, not knowing my real situation, urged me to buy her bread, but I only looked at it hungrily. They whispered among themselves and complained that they had had only bad luck since early morning. I tried and tried, but I could not bear it any longer, so I begged for bread and got some broken pieces. All the discipline and self-respect I had built up in a score of years wept at one corner of my breast.

The bread eased my hunger, and I was able to collect my senses. For fear that the family to whom I owed so much would be in danger and the feeling that the police were following me, I hurried on with all the strength I had. My legs were swelling and blisters on my feet broke and bled. That night I spent on a mountain ridge and tried to satisfy my hunger by chewing grass.

Fortunately for me, several young men escaping the puppet draft into the so-called Volunteer Corps passed by. Like a piece of iron to a magnet, I went up to them. I took out the wrist watch I had carefully concealed, the watch I treasured above all things, and asked them to buy it. They hesitated at first, but finally consented to buy it for 4,000 wons. With that money I bought maize bread and stayed on the mountain three more days. But I felt lonely without the watch.

After three days I was again plagued by hunger, so I went down to a hamlet below. Choosing a house that looked as if it were owned by prosperous people, I went in and got a job as a cook. Yet, to grind the mill, draw water, and tend the children were too much for me. The long days of hunger and coarse food had ruined my constitution and I suffered from dysentery.

Not many days passed before the puppet police had spread out even to this small hamlet, so I moved again. Since I had failed as a cook, I entered a mountain valley and went to a field which few people frequented. I made a foxhole, gathered maize stalks and spread them at the bottom, and spent a number of nights there. I roamed the mountains and fields in search of food. I chewed raw corn and ate raw soybeans. In the nights I fought mosquitoes until my skin was torn to shreds. But always hunger was more difficult to endure than injuries to the body.

One night in the latter part of September I heard loud gunfire. A refugee said that the National army was only five miles away. Without a word I left the place. I dragged my weakened body over hills and across streams to the south, and when I reached a deep mountain recess, I saw at a distance the National Flag flying in the moonlight! My worn-out body seemed to fly. I jumped forward, embraced the flagpole and wept. There was a soldier standing by, and not knowing what to do, I threw my arms around him and cried out loud.

Surveillance and Penalties

The Soviet system of surveillance, devilishly designed to leave nothing unhidden and no one unwatched, was in full operation in Seoul during the summer of 1950. Although the city gave the appearance of usual busy activity there was tension everywhere. Within its limits tens of thousands of its citizens were in hiding. Some, like the minor clerk in the first of the following accounts, went into hiding after arrest and dubious release. Others like the public agency worker whose wife relates the second account, did not wait for inevitable arrest.

> I was arrested by a North Korean plainclothes policeman about ten days after the Communist invasion. I was forced to make a self-criticism in my cell, but as I was a mere clerk without distinction, my confession was only a formality. I was released and ordered to stay at home until summoned again.
>
> As soon as they let me go, I hid in the homes of relatives; I changed homes twice. For three uneasy months I never saw the daylight. I got information through a friend of mine who had a short-wave receiver, and sometimes I came out at night.
>
> I don't know whether I was arrested because my colleagues gave secret information about me, or because of information furnished by some Red living near my house. Somebody, whom my wife dares not identify, came and tried to force her to tell where our two boys were; they were of conscription age and my wife was trying her best to hide them.

> We used to live in an official government residence, but when the invaders came we went into hiding. I was afraid that the Communists would arrest my husband for having been an R.O.K. official, so I kept him in a secret place in the house and allowed no one but myself to open the door for any visitor. We were most afraid from midnight to three in the morning and my husband often hid outside the house during those hours. Once they searched the house for him while he was outside in the bushes.
>
> This went on for three months. We didn't have any money and very little food. Our only source of income was selling clothes. In all the excitement, I did not even notice that I had become pregnant.

Nothing was left to chance. As one citizen of Seoul remarked, "Whenever more than two people gathered, one was surely a spy." The details of the surveillance system were ingeniously contrived and unbelievably complicated. It is possible, nevertheless, to unravel the system to a certain extent, and probably the best starting point is to consider the two most general types of surveillance, that which was done openly and that which was done under cover.

Open surveillance or "watching" was carried on by the security police, by the inspectors, or by the device of self-criticism.

The security police was the force whose job it was to maintain order within the city. Although some degree of secrecy was inherent in their operations, unlike the designated secret police, they were generally readily identifiable and well known. Operatives in this force were assigned all the way from the district to the block unit level. They became the "watch-mongers," constantly on the alert against troublemakers, and highly sensitized to political or ideological defections. The cadre of these police was made up almost entirely of North Korean Communists, who came into Seoul in June elaborately organized and trained and equipped for the job of policing the city. They were not primarily concerned, however, with ordinary violators of the peace, but with enemies of the People's Republic or Communism. Their contacts were informers and other similar agents; they maintained both the intelligence and counter-intelligence systems. As the wife of an R.O.K. official in hiding put it, "Nobody dared to say anything against the Communists, even to his good friend because their watching system was so active and no one could be trusted." They had at their disposal complete dossiers on thousands of South Koreans and there are many accounts of their examinations. In the opinion of the R.O.K. police who succeeded this cadre after the recapture of Seoul, the Communist security police represented the most efficient bureau of the occupation government.

In support of the security police were the inspectors. These were government representatives who moved openly through government offices and the nationalized industries, and to some extent through private business concerns. They were on the alert for suspected inefficiency or mismanagement or malfeasance of any kind. And they were characteristically thorough. They were not above a careful check of the details of bookkeeping, and agricultural inspectors often checked a farmer's reports against an actual count of his poultry or the amount of fruit on his trees. Theoretically, these inspectors were concerned only with efficient operation; it was felt, however, that employees suspected of political deviation were much more likely than others to have their work observed closely. Evidence also indicates that this inspection system was carried into the home as a device for checking on low-level political defection. A doctor, for example, comments, "They searched my house at night several times. I think this was one of their ways to inspect people who ordinarily could not be caught off guard."

Finally, the device of self-criticism or confession provided an excellent source of leads and materials for the security police; it was also a kind of self-surveillance by which the very inside of a person's mind was opened to the officials. The housewife who clearly saw the impossibility of remaining passive in the face of continued self-criticism, is unfortunately by no means an isolated case:

> Although at the beginning of the occupation, I avoided their supervision by pretending to cooperate with them, as time passed, the self-criticism grew more and more difficult to simulate. I should have become either a true cooperator or a rebel if the Communist occupation had continued a little longer.

The secret or undercover surveillance of the city was operated through secret officials and also by means of a device which made a potential policeman of every citizen. Secret police were spaced throughout government agencies, industries, and other services and businesses of importance to the People's Republic. The people did not know who they were and no one in the organization knew who they were. The chief Communists in the organization did not know them; the security police did not know them; the secret police themselves did not know their fellow secret police. Everyone, therefore, was open to suspicion. Everyone must be wary of his fellow workers. There was absolutely no way to tell who might report a political deviation or suspected lack of sympathy with the program of the state to the central government. No one was under any illusion as to the existence of this police force, however, and there were many suspicions of identity. "I have heard people say that the inspector of the block was suspected himself and was being watched by the Communists," said the wife of one professional man. "I understand that there was one person in every office to report secretly on the trend of workers. They called it 'the report on reactionaries,'" reported a professional worker. In the minds of some, there were times when a suspicion would become a certainty. A high school teacher declared "There was a secret agent who took charge of inspection. . . . There was also a secret head of the district besides the formally appointed one." The methods of the secret police were hidden and indirect, but they usually made their arrests during the early morning, and the fate of their victims seldom was made known.

In addition to the official secret police, the way was left open for any individual to operate as a kind of secret policeman. This was known as denunciation; it was encouraged and, if significant, it was apparently rewarded. It could be done in secret, with the identity of the denouncer kept secret, or it could be done in public with the notoriety attractive to some individuals a kind of reward in itself. It furnished an excellent opportunity for paying off old grudges, and was greatly feared as such.

No one could afford an unguarded action. A forty-year-old editor commented bitterly, "Very often one was betrayed by an old friend, so every man kept his secrets to himself." Nor were members of a family unit always safe from each other, in spite of the ties of affection and loyalty in blood relationships. For example, a professor of philosophy and ethics at Chosen Christian College had two daughters, one of whom, unknown to her father, had become a Communist. At the beginning of the occupation of Seoul she at once denounced her father and mother as friendly to America, and both parents were arrested. This was no isolated case.

The Communist treatment of Seoul gave a good indication of their plans for the reorganization of all South Korea. Spread throughout the network of these plans was a system of direct social controls, which in more specific terms might be called a system of rewards and punishments. Some characteristics of this aspect of the Communist plan were plainly discernible even in their brief occupation of this one city.

In the first place, the range of rewards had a tendency to be much wider than the range of punishments. A reward might vary, for instance, from an extra fifty grams of rice to a high post in the hierarchy, but rarely was the lower limit of penalties less than an indeterminate prison sentence with the upper limit death. As a young doctor who was, by virtue of his own illness and the threat of force, in a position to watch the occupation as a staff surgeon in a field hospital, put it succinctly, "The people arrested were murdered or proved missing." This is not to say, of course, that minor punishments such as reduced rations and assignment to road repair work were not meted out. It is simply to emphasize that the system relied more upon inducements than upon deterrents. The out-and-out resister was given short shrift; the potential cooperator was nursed along.

Secondly, the reward system tended to operate in the open whereas the meting out of punishment was increasingly carried on undercover. A teacher described it in a nutshell: "People who do not cooperate simply disappear." This, of course, is in line with the Communist program of "human relations," but more importantly it may possibly indicate the operation of an element of insecurity in Communist thinking. Secret denunciations helped them to protect themselves from the fear of having to admit defections.

The basic pay envelope for cooperation was a government ration card which allowed the holder 500 grams of rice per day plus 200 grams for each member of his family. Some wages were also paid in money depending partly upon the kind of work performed but more basically upon how ideologically correct the recipient was thought to be. The rice ration was the more important, however; as an official bribe it could be adapted to almost any purpose. When the North Korean People's army needed more men, "the family that had a volunteer soldier could get an extra rice ration." Even when the speed-up system was introduced, that is, the completion of a quota of work within a specified time, the positive inducement lay in the rations card, whereas the penalty for non-compliance was a jail sentence or even mysterious disappearance.

For a few who were very cooperative, greater rewards were offered. Teachers, technicians, or artists with a high cooperation rating could always look forward to the possibility of being transferred to North Korea (or even to Russia) for further training and greater opportunities; appointment as a candidate for Party membership was the least that could be expected. These local heroes were widely heralded and publicized, and the machinery for their production was always ready to turn. As one person put it, "Rewarding was exact. It was easy for them to make the low high (and vice versa)."

A third, less tangible type of reward possibly offers a more significant clue to an understanding of Communist psychology. They understood the average person's desire to have approval for behavior and to be a part of things around him and they capitalized on these very basic human characteristics. Although the system was not put into effect in Seoul before the Inchon landings, there is considerable evidence to show that an elaborate scheme for the issuance of "good behavior" certificates and even medals was in hand. Probably considered more important was the lure of status which was attached to membership on certain committees, the attraction of possibly being in on some of the secrets and even of knowing in advance of events that were to happen. To the potential power of such intangible rewards and psychic income the Communists devoted considerable effort and attention.

What happened to the thousands of citizens of Seoul

—marked men, resisters, suspected resisters—who simply disappeared after they were arrested? Many of them were killed. Some were thrown into prison and moved around frequently by night from prison to prison, so that their families could get no word of their whereabouts. Others were taken to North Korea or Manchuria to do manual labor, and some are still there. Still others were put on exhibition, like Kwang-Sun Ke, the industrialist, who gave this account after he was fortunate enough to escape a second arrest:

> On July 15 I was arrested again, and this time by the Political Security Office. On the 17th I was transferred to the West Gate Prison; I was one of the first-class criminals. I was examined five or six times; all examinations took place in the night with beating and torture. When they beat or tortured anyone they did not do it themselves but made some one of their prisoners who had been in the police do it. If the prisoner-torturer showed any mercy, they half killed *him!*
>
> Among the prisoners was Mr. Kyu-Sik Kim [former Minister of Internal Affairs]. They seemed to be after something special from him but he closed his mouth and said nothing. He must have been particularly hated by them, for even when he was returned to his cell he was kept handcuffed in the back. The handcuffs were unlocked only when he ate, and when he slept he could only lie on his side.
>
> In the night of the 25th there were whisperings and loud commands in the cell, and the prisoners were called out singly and by twos. My name was called and when I got outside I saw prisoners lined up in the yard. After being handcuffed we were ordered to march. "Hurry!"

"Hold your tongue!" "Can't you keep the line straight?" The voice of contemptuous scolding, the sound of slapping and the grunt of suppressed pain. It was like a company of prisoners being dragged away into exile in Siberia under the Czarists in Russia.

"Where are we going?" "What's going to happen?" Someone coughed in front.

"Straighten the line, you fool! Move fast!"

"My ankle pains."

"He has sprained his ankle," someone volunteers.

"Shut up. Who told you to talk? It's none of your business to butt in."

Thump, thump, thump; and the sound of pain.

We went to the Seoul station. There was a freight car standing there. We got in like animals—thirty-eight in all, thirty-three Koreans, two Frenchmen, two Frenchwomen and one Englishman. The foreigners looked like priests and nuns. We were guarded by three armed sentries. They were youthful-looking but vicious, and swung the gun barrel upon anyone who made the least whisper.

Meals were of soya beans with a little rice and even that they gave us only twice a day. It was in the middle of the hottest time in summer, and the hardest thing to bear was the thirst. For some unknown reason they never gave any water to prisoners.

The whistle blows. Chug, chug, chug, the train moves on. All of a sudden I get a palpitating sensation in my chest. Am I afraid? I ask myself. I am leaving Seoul. In Seoul are my home and family. When I leave now, I will never see them again. No, it is not fear, but sorrow. . . . The train is climbing around a mountainside. The engine seems short of breath. We must have passed through the neighborhood of Chung-jong Road. Is it due to sadness occasioned by the feeling of leaving Seoul forever that something is rising in my chest and the edges of my eyes are getting hot. . . .

We were on our way to Pyongyang. We got down at Kaesong and spent two nights at the Juvenile Reformatory.

In the daytime we stopped to hide and in the night we proceeded. The air attack of the U.N. forces was getting more and more intense every day. Sometimes we spent the day in some building in an unknown town, and sometimes we hid between the furrows of a maize field.

It was while we were staying in the detention quarters of the Office of Internal Affairs at Pongsan that a large crowd of people rushed to see the place. There was a stream of sightseers all day—for them it was an exhibit of reactionaries from Seoul. Among the sightseers there appeared a vicious burly-looking fellow. He was explaining that as a partisan he had gone down south to oppose the May 15 [1948] general election and that a large number of his comrades had been sacrificed there. He looked through the window and said, "Anyone among you who is a member of the National Assembly raise your hand." One by one the hands raised. "One head, two heads, three heads . . .," the vicious fellow counted to six as if he were counting the number of dogs, and the crowd burst out laughing.

Dae-Sik Chae

The Escape of a Physician

Dr. Chae is probably the only professional man to have survived the September "death march" to Pyongyang.

When Seoul was suddenly occupied by the puppet army, I went into hiding with my wife's people at Anam-Dong. At dawn on July 6 while on a surreptitious visit home I was arrested by members of the Self Government Group. After several days imprisonment in the North Gate Police Station, I was transferred to West Gate Prison, which was crowded with physically and mentally tortured prisoners.

A few days after I went in, a puppet soldier demanded to know if there were any doctors among the prisoners. There was one other doctor besides myself and from that time on we were kept busy attending patients. They kept a close check on everything we did. They watched the medicine supply very carefully, for instance, and were ready to accuse us of ulterior motives in giving out medicine and to beat us with their gun barrels in punishment.

I was kept in West Gate Prison until the middle of September, probably because of my special usefulness to them. But air raids had been getting fiercer every day and the puppet soldiers began to show panic. On the night of September 20 they dragged us all out and began moving. We were tied together by tens in a long column and marched through the streets of Seoul. For each ten prisoners in this death march there were no less than six guards.

Having been locked up so long, the prisoners' thin faces were covered with beards and their lower limbs were so shaky that they found it difficult to walk. All were in the same clothes they had been wearing when they were arrested, and all were without shoes. When anyone fell a guard shouted "Wake up! Do you want to die?" And the unlucky one would be whipped and clubbed with a gun barrel until half dead he picked himself up.

Apparently the puppets were getting ready for street fighting, for as we silently marched on in the darkness, we passed barricades at the entrance of every side street and big crossing. Through Chongno [Bell Street], by Chang Kyong Won [Zoological and Botanical Garden] and through Hei-Wha section, we moved on to Tonam section where I lived. Though it was shrouded in darkness, when I passed my gate I knew that it was my home and my hospital. I had no way of knowing what had happened to my family after my arrest.

We marched for over ten days. Every three days our guards gave us a ball of rice, but never any water. My throat was burning with thirst. When we crossed a ditch the murky water at the bottom was an indescribable temptation. Sometimes during an air raid when we scattered, there would be a ditch nearby and we would fall into it and drink the muddy water, or sometimes we would find ourselves in a vegetable patch and we would pull radishes and chew them dirt and all.

We finally reached Pyongyang on October 7 and were crowded into a small room in a school building. There were so many prisoners that the air was suffocating.

Men, most of them young, were going crazy one after another. An uncontrollable insane laugh would bring the guard's gun barrel on the unfortunate one's head, and he would be dragged away, never to return. Fear and foreboding weighed upon us like a stone.

Three days passed and then in the night we were again dragged out, two thousand of us. Bound together again by tens, the long serpentine line headed north.

The throb of a motor told us that a truck was going with us. When I learned that the truck was filled with spades and pickaxes my hair bristled toward heaven and a cold wind whirled in my bosom. As the procession entered a mountain valley I knew we were going to be massacred. Death was just one step ahead. I had the feeling that my blood was suddenly running backward in my veins.

Luckily the rope that bound me was thin. Even now I cannot tell where I got the tremendous strength, but once, twice, three times, I put my whole strength into breaking it. When it finally parted I fell to the ground pulling those next to me down with me.

"Which fellow is it?" shouted a guard as his rifle barked.

Fright pulled the others to their feet, but I crept away into the darkness and lay flat and still in the weeds. My chest was about to burst and there was a noise in my ears like escaping steam.

An hour must have passed before I first raised my head and looked around. Aside from the occasional fluttering of mountain birds there was nothing in evidence. I got up, but fell back again at a sudden pain in my wrist.

When I touched it, my hand became slippery with blood where the skin had been badly torn when I broke the rope.

As I lay on the ground and looked up at the stars in the sky, tears filled my eyes. I suppose this was a sign of weakness, but I could not control them. "Must go south, must go south," I told myself. Once again I rose and began to walk over the hills, through the fields and across streams until ahead of me in the distance I saw a grayish white streak. Teadong River!

The problem now was how to cross this river safely. Just as I squatted down among the weeds to consider the possibilities along came two or three wagons. I quickly wedged myself in between them unnoticed apparently by any of the drivers.

Dawn was beginning to break as we reached the river and the sentry shouted, "Who goes there?" "Returning wagon from requisition service," one of the drivers answered and the sentry seemed satisfied. We crossed the river without a mishap.

Once on the opposite shore, I slid away from the wagons and hid myself between the furrows in a field. By this time the sun was above the hilltop. I thought then it would be foolish to try to cover any ground in daylight so I spent a long day between the furrows and did not bestir myself again until it was quite dark.

I kept to the hills in order to avoid towns as much as possible. I must have walked for an hour when I heard someone shout, "Who goes there?" Instinctively I fell flat. Then, above the rustling sound of the high grass on the slope below someone answered, and I soon saw that he was a puppet soldier with a burp gun.

After a while I crept up the slope in the opposite direction. When I reached the top an astonishing sight was awaiting me. Unwittingly I had crept up to an assembly area of puppet tanks. In all haste I went in the opposite direction. This experience made me realize that night travel and mountain roads were dangerous and from that time on I kept to level ground and traveled in the daytime.

Two days later I became conscious of the fact that a strange man was following me. I walked on for a while and then I saw a flock of chickens scratching the ground in a vegetable garden. This gave me an idea. I began to chase the chickens from the garden, brandishing a stick and shouting, "Shoo, you confounded chickens! What do you mean by ruining the garden?"

The man continued on his way out of sight. I thought I had convinced him that I was the owner of the garden, but as I looked back when leaving the village he was still following me. The need to lose him was urgent. I zigzagged my course at random and at twilight hid myself in a field of maize. I did not know how many days it had been since I had eaten a meal, but in the field I fell over and almost lost consciousness from hunger. I plucked and chewed an ear of maize, but it was not satisfying. A little later I heard a slight movement near my head. It was a field mouse. Taking careful aim I struck it with my stick. Then calmly I ate this little field mouse.

At the time I was arrested, I managed to take with me a quantity of codeine, intending to destroy myself if I had to. As things turned out, instead of destroying me it helped me to continue to live. In a village that I passed through I came upon a man who was coughing a great deal. I offered him some of the codeine and it relieved his cough. This cure was soon noised about and as a result I sold all the codeine I had for about 1,000 wons. I now had money to go to Nam-chon. To my great joy when I arrived there I found our Republican army and the U.N. forces with our national flag flying. When I saw the flag I raised my stick in salute and shouted "Mansei." Then I wept.

Sang-Sup Um

The Escape of a Public Prosecutor

Sang-Sup Um was the former public prosecutor for Seoul.

On the 27th of June I sent my family to our home town of Songjongni. In the evening of the same day I started south by car with the Minister of Law. Later, on the train to Mokpo, I decided to get off at Iri and stay there for awhile and watch the turn of events. Ten days later I heard that the National Assembly had come down to Chonju and I went there. During the five days I spent in Chonju the war situation changed rapidly for the worse. The Kumkang defense line of Taejon broke and there was nothing to stop the puppet army from rushing down like a pack of wolves. Disheartened, I journeyed wearily on foot to Kwangju. From Kwangju I went to Songjongni and found that my family had had a hard time in getting out of Seoul. The enemy rushed down on the southwestern provinces like a tide. I decided to send my family to my father-in-law's home village in Imja Island of Mu-an County and to go myself to Pusan. But the approach of the enemy was so rapid I had to follow my family to Imja Island. As the boat sailed toward the island, the unfeeling sea gulls wheeling in the sky seemed to accentuate my despair.

Five days after we arrived on the island we learned that nearly all the southern provinces had fallen into the hands of the enemy, and already even in this comparatively remote islet, a body called the People's Committee was in operation. It was impossible to find a safe refuge on such a small island, for I could not hide without arousing suspicion.

When, after much, much thinking, I decided that I must escape from the island, it was already too late. Sailings were frozen and the organized net was beginning to spread throughout the island.

As a former Public Prosecutor and a present member of the National Assembly, I knew I must attempt to avoid detection, so I tried to hide myself in the house of a relative, but this too proved to be fruitless. One day a crowd of puppets kicked open the door, rushed into my place of hiding, and in the twinkling of an eye arrested me. They were so sure of finding me I think there must have been an informer.

I knew they were taking those whom they arrested to the beach and shooting them, and I expected to meet the same fate. To my surprise instead, I was imprisoned in the warehouse of the Financial Guild of Imja Island, which was used as the jail of the People's Committee. Once every few days I was brought out and subjected to senseless examinations and torture. The most difficult thing to endure was when they beat my shin bones with a big club. Yet, even while they were doing it I felt somehow that they were not going to kill me. It was strange. Maybe they had been ordered by their superiors not to kill me because I was a member of the National Assembly, but if this were the case, the puppet crowd in the island didn't approve of the verdict. They looked at me with disgust and never ceased to hurl insults.

About this time a misfortune fell upon my family. Our year-old baby got sick and a few days afterward I heard that he had died of a contagious disease. Two other children, the three-year-old and the nine-year-old died a few days later. With the death of her children and with the threat of death hanging over her imprisoned husband, my wife went half insane in the space of a few days. I myself seemed to be going crazy in that lonely dark warehouse where only the sound of wind and waves could be heard. In addition to this mental torture, I became physically ill, and as my body became more emaciated the illness grew worse.

Through the efforts of my wife a certain person of good will was successful in intervening on my behalf and I received permission to be out on bail for five days. The sight of me was another terrible shock to my wife. I tried to console her and give her courage. "We cannot undo what has happened. We are in the hands of fate. Whatever happens let us meet it with strength."

During those five days, through the tender devotion of my wife and a strong constitution, I recovered somewhat. When the five days had passed I was not ordered back to my prison. I could not understand this, for at this time the fortunes of the war had not turned. Then I was told that the police had gone to Mokpo to receive orders, and I determined to hide myself before they returned. I went to a secret room in a relative's house which was so designed that no observation could detect it.

A few days after I went into this room the island was caught in a great wave of new fear. The police orders demanded a final liquidation. Arrests were made and massacres were carried out before the people's very eyes. More than half the population of some hamlets was wiped out. Shooting was not the only method of killing, they killed by stabbing, clubbing, and burying alive. Often they threw the bodies into the sea.

One night, while I hid in the secret room, I suddenly heard shots being fired from the back of the house. Soon after there was a light tap on the door and the voice of my landlady warned, "There is an investigation. Be careful!"

I wanted to be careful, but how? All I could do was try to suppress my very breath and sit still.

Then I heard footsteps and voices. There must have been more than ten of them. They had surrounded the house and had begun seaching it. As the footsteps neared my room, my breathing stopped and my hair bristled toward the sky. Shall I go out? Would it not be better to go out? I wanted to shout, "I am here! Sang-Sup Um is here!" I wanted to laugh in their faces.

I waited one second, two, three. Then, just as I was about to kick open the door and rush out, the footsteps moved on. Other footsteps followed but they, too, passed me by. Soon afterwards I heard two shots, and cries of "Here!" "Come!" Then the sound of something striking and of a woman's cry of terror. They had found the woman who had been hiding in the house behind us and immediately clubbed her to death.

Some ten days after this night, on October 19, the Liberator Company of our Republic army landed on the island. I was free again but the nightmare of the last weeks would not leave me and I could not believe it.

Institutional Reforms

Wherever the process of sovietization has been systematically started or actually consummated, it has always been accompanied by plans for far-reaching institutional changes, and Seoul, during the summer of 1950, was no exception. In respect to the home, private property, freedom of speech and religion, the Communists were already, in this first phase of the creation of a satellite state, beginning to introduce specific "reforms." The home, especially insofar as it symbolized the tradition of father authority and the subordination of women, automatically became an enemy of the state. Private property, since it has high visibility as the seat of economic power, and hence of political power, constituted an equally important threat. Freedom of speech obviously had to be curtailed, and acknowledgment of any power greater than the Communist Party had to be eliminated.

Apparently little was done about the pressing issues of religion during the three months of occupation. The confiscation of church property and the removal or liquidation of religious leaders were both motivated primarily by immediate practical needs. Church property was taken over for military purposes; church leaders were eliminated largely because of the existence of their following. Issues involving a conflict between church and state were obviously in the wind, but they were not specifically articulated during the short three-month period. In contrast, right at the beginning freedom of speech and inquiry were immensely restricted by the close control of communications, by surveillance, by the technique of self-criticism, and through the remaking of the school system. The blueprint called for additional measures of even more drastic nature but the time simply had not come for their implementation. The three examples, consequently, which best illustrate the developing program of institutional reform are found in the home, especially in the position of women, in the factories, and on the land, especially with reference to the question of ownership.

The authority of the father in Korea is traditional. He demands obedience and reverence from every member of the family. His behavior is detached and arbitrary. He orders the flogging of his children, chooses wives and occupations for his sons, and ordains a strictly different standard of morality and social behavior for the women of his family. The Communists attacked this established tradition by strengthening the power and extending the opportunities of women and children. Attendance in the Women's Alliance and the Youth Alliance was as nearly compulsory as it could be made, and membership was pronounced a great honor.

In the Women's Alliance, women were taught that in every respect they were the equal of men, and appointments and employment were to be open equally to them insofar as they could do the work. Concubinage and prostitution were labeled social evils, and the power of the Alliance backed up the women whose husbands committed those evils. The propaganda against concubinage apparently made a deep impression in Seoul.

"If the Women's Alliance accused a man of having a concubine, he was put into jail," reported a Seoul husband with obvious respect. Furthermore, the Communists opened the way to easier divorces, apparently adopting the North Korean law that if a husband asked for a divorce and received it, the woman was entitled to half his property; but if the woman asked for and received the divorce, she was entitled to *all* the property. Finally, they appointed at least one woman to every People's Committee, opened other political and official jobs to women, and encouraged them to go into industry and business and even into hard labor—as one woman reported, "digging ditches and carrying ammunition."

In the Youth Alliance, the Communists taught the importance of young men and women in the Party program. The Alliance not only frequently kept young people away from home but also taught that the Party's claim was superior to that of the father. For the first time in the family history many a son or daughter must have picked a political argument with a thunderstruck father. Many members must have been assigned also to spy on their own families.

The results of such a policy are clearly evident in North Korea where there had been time for it to develop. Women in the North held jobs of honor, worked at employment hitherto denied them, sometimes went around calling each other *tong-mu* (comrade). Both women and children spent at meetings a number of hours which formerly would have been spent in the home. In South Korea, the events of three short months undoubtedly accelerated the process of change in the home and the authority of the father, and there is no doubt that the change would have continued at a faster rate if the occupation had been continued.

Although the nationalization of industry had been one of the strident promises shouted by the Communists upon their entry into Seoul in late June, their record of fulfillment during the three months that followed was poor. Save for the major transportation and communication facilities and a few heavy industries, the nationalization program scarcely emerged from the planning stage. This is not to say, however, that such a situation would have continued for long. The North Korean story was ready to be retold in the South, and the key to their economic plans, apart from the obviously crucial question of agricultural land reform, is to be found in their attitude toward small business, which in a relatively non-industrial country like Korea represents most industrial activity.

Although land had been redistributed in North Korea and seemed to be on its way to becoming collectivized and although many industries were nationalized, still no move seems to have been made toward the nationalizing of small business. It was soon discovered, however, that the familiar Communist tactics were operating, as the following account by a Hamhung merchant shows:

> One of the important policies of the North Koreans was to suppress big business, but in their propaganda they promised to encourage individual business. At first I was deceived by this propaganda, and with all the money I had and some that my relatives were willing to invest, I asked for permission to establish a factory. They not only gave me permission, but told me if I needed some

materials they would supply them. Encouraged by this, I started to build the factory. The first month's tax was 5,000 won and I thought that was not so bad. But in the second month they told me I would have to pay 10,000. In the third and fourth months the tax increased to 15,000 and then 20,000. Altogether I paid 50,000 in taxes and by the fourth month my capital was gone. Although my factory had been built, I had nothing left to run it with, and the Communists had a good excuse to confiscate it. I lost all of my own money as well as that of my relatives.

The tricky method of squeezing out investment capital, and of creating state-owned stores to try to undersell and supplant privately owned stores, is the same general kind of operation as first to confiscate land from the large owners and then tax it away from the small ones. There was a heavy tax also on merchants.

The only possible conclusion from this and corresponding evidence is that small business, like private industry in manufacturing and agriculture, was also on the way out, but the Communists were willing to postpone and compromise until the right moment came.

A refugee from North Korea reported that he had this explanation from high authority:

Beginning in 1946 large-scale industries were nationalized and we could expect that small enterprises would also be nationalized gradually. There seem to be two important reasons why the People's Republic permitted small enterprises, according to what I heard directly from a high-ranking officer of the Communist Party: (1) if they nationalized all the industries immediately, they would not only induce the dissatisfaction of the middle class citizens, but would also cause conflict with farmers who were closely attached to the land, and this would be detrimental to the process of revolution; and (2) they believed that it was not necessary for them to eliminate small enterprises because the small ones would disperse themselves. National factories could get raw materials preferentially and could purchase them more cheaply. Also, profits from the national factories would be used for the welfare of the laborers, whereas the profits in a private factory would be exploited by the managers. Therefore, since the worker's income in a private factory would be less than in a national one, the laborer's effectiveness also would be lowered. Finally, the private factory would be absorbed eventually into the national anyway, so there was no need to eliminate them.

In broader and more general terms, this is the analysis given by a university professor who had been watching the process for five years:

> Of course there is some logic in the nationalization of industry. People may not like to live under the society of capitalism, but the Communist plan of nationalization of industry did not spring from the rejection of capitalism itself; it was meant to drive out the ready-made power in Korea. The great doctrine of Communism is first of all to destroy all the established organizations, powers, and ideas of the society which they invade.

The master plan for sovietizing a satellite such as Korea, it appears, is a long-range one. At the beginning they find it necessary, of course, to destroy existing leadership and what the professor calls "ready-made power," but the long-range objective is to supplant the local order, customs, and traditions with their own system.

If Korea is a fair example they are willing to go about this slowly; stateways can be changed quickly, but the part of the culture which is closer to folkways and custom must be handled more carefully. They first calculate, therefore, how much dislocation the society can stand at a given time, and try to bring about change always in the desired direction but at the optimum rate. The nationalizing of small business, like the collectivizing of land, comes later in the schedule. Meanwhile, the small businessman will be tolerated as long as he is useful, but even during the period of usefulness, crippling taxes and state competition are preparing the way for the next stage in the master plan.

The Republic of South Korea had just passed the Land Reform Law in June of 1950 and no actual redistribution had taken place. It is surprising, consequently, that the Communists failed to seize the opportunity provided by an existing law to exploit the situation and to effect redistribution on a large scale. The North Korean model was already established, the machinery for its operation in South Korea was set up and well oiled, yet at most, not more than ten per cent of South Korea was actually redistributed between June and September.

The Communist organizational plan for land reform can perhaps best be understood by comparing several of its salient features with the South Korean plan. In general terms, the R.O.K. law provided for the government purchase of all privately owned land of more than two and one-half acres, but this depended to some extent upon the location and the quality of the land in question. Such issues, as well as the general administration of the law, were placed in the hands of locally elected committees of seven members—one land owner, and six tenants or owner-tenants.

In contrast, the North Korean plan called for all land to be taken over and divided equally, but provided for a tax structure which, of course, was tantamount to payment over a period of time. Its administration was also in the hands of a local committee but with important differences. The chairman of the committee was the local Communist Party secretary whose administrative aide was a carefully screened mayor. These two then appointed the other members of the committee and could decide which individuals were to receive the best plots of land. On this point, the available evidence indicates that the best land was given to two classes of people: (1) staunch supporters of the Party, and (2) the poorest and most tractable elements of the tenant class.

Furthermore, according to the South Korean plan, the new owners of the redistributed land were to make payments over a five-year period by turning in fifteen per cent of the main crop each year, whereas the Communist plan called for a twenty-seven per cent tax on all crops. It was widely estimated that this could have actually reached a total of as much as seventy per cent (for the tax was to be fixed according to the quality of the crop), but since most crops had not matured by September when the Communists were thrown back, the evidence is far from complete.

The occupying authorities also had an elaborate paper plan for exploiting the existing South Korean Farmers' Finance Association, which permeated down to the village level. And while they went so far as to put their own personnel in the key positions, nothing actually was done to put either the credit or marketing machinery in motion. That the Reds planned to do this is abundantly clear, despite the fact that their ultimate objective was collectivization. It is a good illustration of their ability to compromise and to proceed along the most expedient lines without any overt sacrifice of long-range principles or goals. The essential ideological argument, of course, was that the land was to be redistributed "free and equally," in sharp contrast to the pre-invasion South Korean system which would "continue to protect vested interests along both class and property lines."

It appears that, in general, the idea of the Communist land reform was welcomed during the very early phases of the occupation—especially, of course, by the tenants—and that only gradually did actual experience begin to create a different attitude. As the collection of the many unannounced "extras" began, the common complaint was: "In addition to the tax-in-kind, there might be frequent collections of so-called patriotic crops. How we farmers got along after paying tax-in-kind and the patriotic collections!"

The most frequent objection, eventually, centered upon the amount of the actual tax which was imposed. Even though the people of Seoul may have had little personal experience with agricultural problems, they were both incensed and apparently well informed on this situation. The word of the farmers' plight had traveled far and fast, and after the occupation comments such as the following were frequently heard from non-farmers:

> They collect more than seventy per cent of the output in spite of their announced twenty-five per cent.

> At the (early) harvest season when the individual amount of tax-in-kind was estimated, the farmers were seized by terror. Not only because the tax-in-kind was imposed on all products, but because the procedure was so formidable that the farmers couldn't bear it.

> The farmers (apparently) rather preferred to have no land at all since after all their trouble most of the harvest would be requisitioned.

But however much criticism may have been generated against the land distribution program and its implementation, the fact remains that the Communists were working from a master plan in which they had both confidence and considerable experience.

In respect to the other institutional features of South Korean society, approximately the same kind of picture emerges. In some instances, as in the case of the Ministry of Communications, considerable actual reorganization took place. In others, in the Ministry of Justice for instance, the extent to which the plans were carried out represented only a token kind of control.

But in all cases the organizational plans for the sovietization of South Korea were well laid and the ground well prepared. That the Communists expended the greater part of their efforts during these critical first months on those organizational aspects having to do with control systems and the dissemination of the ideological line may therefore constitute a significant clue to their long-range plans for other countries and for other times.

Sin-Duk Whang

What Happened to a Teacher

Sin-Duk Whang was presumably the only survivor of one group taken to Pyongyang during the late summer.

It seems unreal to me to be alive and even more unreal to sit in my home and write about my escape from Pyongyang. Whenever this doubt comes to me, even in sleep, I get up with a shudder, open the window, and look around in order to reassure myself that this is really my home in our own town. I am alive. I have indeed escaped and returned to Seoul and can sleep peacefully in my own room.

Yet when I think of my compatriots who were taken away in captivity by the Red Satans and are not yet heard from, it seems that my chest is going to burst. I have had the bitter taste because I was one of them, and at times I have the guilty feeling that only I have escaped with my life and returned.

Frankly, I did not believe the puppet army would occupy our capital so quickly. We heard the booming of the guns, but the report of the recapture of Uijongbu reassured us. However, as I look back I realize that even if I had known the real situation beforehand there would have been nothing else for me to do but wait and try to go through it. What else could I have done with a large family and no money?

It was terrible the morning of June 28th, after a night of anxiety and turmoil, to find the city in the hands of the puppets. I spent the first three weary days in the house, and then I began to hear that through the manipulation of the so-called "people's courts," our people were being murdered all about. Fear and uncertainty were increasing day by day. For my part I had the comforting thought that an insignificant school person like myself would probably be overlooked. But that showed how lacking I was in an understanding of the character of the cruel puppets.

On the unforgettable 25th of July a strange young man called about noon. Without answering my question about where he came from, he insisted that I should write a confession and a statement of surrender. I was inwardly afraid, but outwardly I said calmly that I would think about it, and barely succeeded in sending him away. It was then that I began to think about going into hiding, but to go into hiding is no easy matter when one's family is large.

A few days later while I was procrastinating, he came again, this time with an entirely different attitude and demanded that I surrender. His face was flushed with anger as he threatened me in insulting language. I could hardly control my own rising anger and I resolved that even if it meant death I would not go in hiding. Once the resolution was made, I was no longer afraid. I absolutely refused to write the surrender statement. He just looked at me strangely and went away, but in the afternoon a man from the Office of Internal Affairs came and took me away.

The members of my family came out of the gate to the entrance of the street and wept as I left. I could not help my inner sorrow, but I would not let them see it. I told them that I had done no wrong and that I fully expected to return soon. Then I sent them back in the house.

They took me first to the Political Security Bureau and kept me there for about three days. After that I was taken to three or four places which I did not know.

On the not-to-be-forgotten July 30th I was put in a covered truck.

"Where are we going?" I asked.

"Pyongyang," was the laconic answer. Seventy-nine of us were being carried away in two trucks. Among them were Mr. Dong-Won Kim; Professor Choon-Ho Lee; Mr. Bung-Jun Kim; President Sang-Yum Hyon of the Korean University; Messrs. Hyong-Won Kim, Myong-Kyun Koh, and Yang-Myong Hong. There were also thirty-two foreigners who looked like White Russians and priests. I was the only woman. With ten fierce puppet guards for each truck, we left Seoul in the evening twilight.

The truck rumbled on all night. We were not allowed to say a word, and the puppet soldiers employed all sorts of threats and insults to torture us. "Now, when we get to such and such a place we will shoot so and so, and at such and such a place everybody will get 'people's court trial,' " the puppets sneered. Every time the trucks stopped at some town whose name we did not know the thought of instant death recurred. The foreign priests mumbled with bent heads, seemingly offering up prayers.

Even in this condition we suffered unbearable hunger. We were not even given the ball of boiled barley which we used to get in Seoul once a day. We were all getting numb and on the verge of blackout.

About noon the next day, that is the 31st, we were ordered to alight for the first time. It was at Namchon in Whanghae Province. We were led into a building on the wall of which was a sign "The People's Court." The thought of this misfortune overwhelmed everybody; it seemed that death was falling right in front of the feet. Some put their palms together, others made the Sign of the Cross, and still others recited their last will.

Entering a room we found food; but thinking it to be the last meal, we found it difficult to swallow. When the meal was over a member of the Office of Internal Affairs came in and harangued on the supposed virtues of northern politics and the alleged evils of southern politics. His talk had no semblance of logic. After the harangue was over, much to our surprise we left Namchon.

We arrived at Pyongyang at about 8 o'clock that evening and immediately they pulled out Mr. Dong-Won Kim, saying that he was going to be shot at once. After that all of us were put in a pitch-dark room. Again the uncertainty of our lives ran a race with time. Even now I can hear the sound of coughs, sighs and prayers in that black, dark room.

After about an hour we were called out one by one to be examined. When the examinations were over we were made to hide in the covered trucks again and, crossing the Taedong River, were taken to a prison which was called the Reformatory Center. I was taken to the women's cell and was astonished to find there Mrs. Sung-Ho Pak, Miss Gladys Koh, Miss Jung-Hi Lee (an aviatrix), and a policewoman from Inchon.

Our meals were a mixture of millet, maize and soya beans and there were no special examinations. After about three days I was again taken aboard a truck, with about 30 of those who had been brought up from Seoul, among whom was Mr. Sang-Chun Suh.

We were imprisoned in a place that looked like a school building and were examined there. Those who were examined first were young literary men, and as soon as the examinations were over they disappeared.

My turn came after about one week. When ordered to write down the names of government officials whom I knew, I said that I had been away in America and I knew no one. Then the examiner brought forth a card I had addressed to Col. Ben C. Limb, the Minister of Foreign Affairs, and said with rolling eyes, "Even with this, would you say that you do not know anyone?" It was a card I had sent to Minister Limb upon my return home. Then he asked what I did and whom I had met in America and I said that I met no one in particular. At that, he produced a photograph of me taken with Dr. P. O. Chough. I was really surprised, for they had a photograph of me I had never seen myself.

"We make detailed investigations like this, and you had better make a truthful confession." The examining officer was razor-like in his interrogation, and thoroughly enjoyed the situation. He spent long hours in sweating me with questions regarding Dr. Chough, the United Nations, the object of organizing the Korean National Independence-Expediting Women's Association, the reason why the trusteeship was opposed, etc.

I was examined once a day for a number of days. During that time I saw many friends and acquaintances brought in for examination, as well as at least three hundred others. When the examinations were finally over I was again taken to the Pyongyang prison.

As the air raids of the U.N. forces increased in intensity the puppet government began to show panic. This was during the first ten days of October. Yet there was no way of our knowing that Inchon had been taken and Seoul recaptured by the Republican and U.N. forces.

In the dead of night on October 10th we were suddenly dragged out and made to walk to an unknown destination. From the sky an intense air raid opened up, and the whirring of the planes, the firing of the anti-aircraft guns, and the explosions of the bombs and shells made such a din that it seemed that heaven and earth were crashing.

As the endless column marched on, a tremendous explosion made us look back and we saw a sea of fire. Maybe it was the prison we had just left behind.

Just then there was a sudden brilliant flare over our heads, and the puppet soldiers who were driving us dived into the foxholes on the side of the street and told us to follow them.

Instantly I made a decision: "I am going to die anyhow, so I will run as fast as I can." A bomb fell right in front of us with a big explosion that shook the earth. With extraordinary exertion I ran in the opposite direction of the foxhole. "A runaway!" the puppets called, and bullets flew over my head. I fell flat and began creeping. After some struggle I got into a broken-down air-raid shelter and hid myself.

When the air raid was over everything was shrouded in complete darkness and silence. Then a muffled voice was heard and then other voices, followed by five or six shots. They must be looking for me! I was never so overcome by fright as at this time. My teeth chattered and my legs shook violently.

Soon I could no longer hear them and I crept out of the shelter, for I felt there was no safety for me there.

The day would soon break and I had to find safety. I walked on into the dark for what must have been about three miles. Day was dawning when I found myself in a quiet farming village. I knocked at a door and explained that I was an escapee from an air raid. They did not suspect me and gave me breakfast.

From there I went to the house of a member of our school staff at Kum-jei and hid myself for about a week. In the meantime Pyongyang was captured by our Republican soldiers and the U.N. forces.

Yung-Sang Kim

What Happened to a Newspaperman

Yung-Sang Kim was an avowed anti-Communist who outwitted the Security Police.

On June 28 I stayed at home in Chebu-Dong, dispirited by the indescribable confusion outside where murder and plundering went on even in broad daylight. The noise of the puppet troops continued all day, and I put my books and papers in order, expecting disaster at any moment.

It came the very next night when six or eight ruffians scaled the garden walls and rushed in. Some had rifles, some had Japanese daggers, others had clubs. They looked like a band of robbers but they called themselves the Volunteer Guards. In the early stages the Volunteer Guards limited their arrests and kidnaping to members of the South Korean Youth Organization and the police and armed forces. With their limited ability, they only knew how to deal with those they felt were active and clear-cut opponents.

They bound me immediately and began searching the house. Then: "You are a newspaperman, aren't you?" one of them asked me. There was no use in trying to deny it. They took me outside, my wife following and weeping but to no avail. I was being taken to the hill behind Chebu-Dong—I was on the road to death. At the moment my mind was extraordinarily clear: there was no sadness, no surprise, no fear. I was going calmly to receive the bullet.

But at the top of the hill instead of shooting me, they

took me to a villa and put me in a corner room. As my eyes got more accustomed to the darkness I saw there was another person in the room, who turned out to be a member of the staff of the Youth Organization.

Some hours later we were taken out singly and questioned. It was plain that our questioners were ignorant so I decided to counter their questions with some of my own. "For what reason have you arrested me? What crime is there in being a newspaperman?" I asked them.

For every question they asked me, I had one for them. My persistence may have been effective. At any rate, I was released at dawn. As I went down the hill and walked toward my home everything seemed to have changed. But it was not my surroundings that had changed, but I, myself. I had been close to death and it was as if I were returning home after a long trip.

The light was still dim when I reached home and shook the gate.

"Who's that?" called my wife.

"It's me. Open the gate, hurry and open the gate!" I answered.

"Who are you? Whoever you are, give me your name."

"Are you out of your mind? Why should you ask your own husband his name? Hurry and open the gate!"

Cautiously then she looked through the crack and then in great joy and surprise threw open the gate. She told me that she thought I had been killed and that when she heard someone at the gate she had been afraid it was my murderer who had returned to rob the house.

After that I was more careful and for a while hid myself in the back room day and night. Yet, I found it impossible to stay in all the time without knowing what was going on, so I began to go out occasionally and very carefully during the daytime.

One day as I was walking along the street with a friend of mine someone struck me on the shoulder. Turning I saw two strange men. "Aren't you a newspaperman of the *Seoul News?*" one of them asked. Again denial was useless. He told me to come with them for a moment. I demanded he tell me who he was but I only got a brusque "You will know when we get there." The suddenness of the thing took my breath away and I followed him without a word.

Making several turns through back alleys he took me to a dim-looking two-story house in Nakwon-Dong. Neither the fellow who took me there nor the ones in the house looked like the regular puppet police, however poor a showing the latter make. First they asked me to kneel down on the floor and began to ask me irrelevant questions, then they told me to get up and took me outside again.

As if I had never been in danger before, my heart sank. Having once been dragged into the hills, I did not know where they would take me this time. Common sense told me that if they were regular police, even though they were puppets, they would have some legal basis for their action. On the other hand if they were members of a suddenly formed private organization they would be as unpredictable as a baby with a razor.

Suddenly, as we were passing the Whashin Department Store, I ignored "face" and simply sat down on the sidewalk.

"Why on earth are you sitting down?" one of them asked, and rolled his eyes.

"I want to know where you are taking me. If you must arrest me, take me to the Chongno Police Station which is near."

"You crazy loon! Think we'll take you where you want to go? Stop your impertinence and get up." Then he kicked me.

Helplessly I got up and followed him to the West Gate Internal Affairs Office, where he sat me in front of a desk. After a while someone appeared behind the desk, looked at me hard, and asked, "Don't you know me?" He was wearing dark glasses and I did not recognize him.

"I cannot remember," I said.

"Why can't you remember?" He took off his glasses. "Now can you remember?"

My mouth flew open. I recognized him as an employee in the propaganda bureau of a certain political party; he had worked there after the 1945 liberation. As a newspaper reporter I had had frequent contact with him and we were on familiar terms with one another.

"How long it has been!" I extended my hand half in diplomacy and half in real pleasure. But he did not seem to have any idea of shaking hands with me.

"Did you know when I was getting acquainted with you that I was a Communist agent working the propaganda bureau of the political party?" he asked.

"I did not know. How could I know?"

"Do you realize that you have been a rightist newspaperman and that your crime is great in having supported the reactionary politics?"

I could not answer. I silently gazed at his face. It seemed incredible to me that this man would brag to a prisoner that he had been a Communist agent while working in the propaganda bureau of another political party.

He asked many random questions of me, and finally turned me over to a plainclothes policeman to be taken over to the Political Security Office.

The streets were dark when we came out and got in the car. The office where I was to be taken was next to the National Library, but the driver and the police seemed to be unfamiliar with the streets of Seoul. After turning around a good deal through the Namdae-Mun [South Gate] and Sowha Boulevard and wasting much time, the car reached the Political Security Office.

They took me upstairs and told the man behind the desk that I was a prisoner from the West Gate Internal Affairs Station. The man's answer surprised my guard, for he said, "No prisoner can be accepted here. We deal only with those who voluntarily surrender."

"Then what can we do with this prisoner?"

"Try the office downstairs," answered the man.

I was taken downstairs, but the answer was the same. There was nothing for us to do but leave. It was nearly one o'clock in the morning and there we were on the street outside the Security Office. This was really a dilemma for the police. After much thinking, he asked me, "Can you go to your house if you try?"

"I can," I quickly answered.

"Then go, and come at nine o'clock tomorrow morning to the West Gate Station."

"I will do that," I replied.

"Then hurry and go."

But as I started to leave an important fact dawned upon me. It was already past one o'clock in the morning, and curfew started at nine P.M. After that hour Seoul was a place of terror. I had seen persons on emergency errands shot down in the streets. My mind went blank for a second. Then I said, "It can't be done. Unless you take me in the car to my house I will be shot, for the night is too late." I kept insisting that I would not go unless they took me in the car, and if I did not go, the police would have to spend the night with me in the street. It was plain that the thought did not appeal to him, for he finally consented to drive me home. However, he made me get out at the entrance of Chebu-Dong; beyond that, he contended, it was impossible to go.

Finding further argument useless, I left the car when we were about two hundred yards from my home. I did not know if I could cover that distance without being shot. I took one step and stopped, then two steps, and cold sweat broke out on my forehead, for I heard shots being fired not far away. If I was discovered now by the puppet soldiers, I would be felled on the spot. One slow step followed another as I strained to see ahead of me. Then something, perhaps the shots, awakened the dogs in the neighborhood and they began to bark insanely. I kept going, but slowly, and when the shots came closer I fell flat and waited for them to pass or to stop. At the pace of a measuring worm, I finally reached home.

In the morning I went again to the West Gate Station and again to the Security Office. After three days of examination I was released and sent home. I went into hiding fast. If I had not, I would certainly have been arrested again. I would not have seen this happy day, nor would I have again enjoyed a life of freedom under our national flag.

Hei-Sook Pak

What Happened to an Actress

Despite an extraordinary escape, the family and friends of Hei-Sook Pak did not learn of her survival until several weeks after the re-occupation of Seoul.

The chaotic night of June 27! At ten o'clock that night, with the booming of the big guns coming louder and closer minute by minute, I said goodbye to my husband and set out to cross the Han River with my daughter, Chinyung.

My husband, Dr. Kim, was a medical doctor and had nothing to do with politics, so he felt that it was safe for him to stay in Seoul. But since I was connected with movies, radio and the theatre, I did not think I would be allowed to share his safety.

We thought the trouble would soon be over and that after a short separation the family would have a joyful reunion. How little we knew what lay in store for us.

Crossing the Han River, my daughter and I joined Chief Prosecutor Ik-Chin Kim's family in their car. There were five of us—Chief Prosecutor Kim, his wife, their daughter, and we two.

We spent the night in Anyang and went down to Suwon the next day. Then, as the puppet army rolled on like the incoming waves, we moved farther south, first to Chonan, then to Kongju, and again, by July 12, to Puyan and Hogsan, where many of my in-laws live. We stayed with them and their relatives in nearby villages of Puyan, a few days in each place.

Ik-Chin Kim had stopped at Taegu where the government had gone, and our party had been reduced to four, all women.

Realizing that Puyan was also in danger, we thought of moving either to Taejon or to Taegu, but there was the Inchon River to cross. Then we thought of going to Puyan District Seat, but there was the Pangma River. We were blocked.

I was traveling under an assumed name, So-Yawn Pak, but I couldn't change my face. Through movies my face had become known far and wide; people stared at me and easily identified me. Although I walked along the country roads in a hempen dress with an old-fashioned hair-do, still some of the refugees would stare at me and whisper. I tried to overhear what they said:

"She is a movie actress."

"Yes! She played the mother's part!"

They did not mean any harm, but it was a danger signal and I felt very nervous. I knew then that I couldn't stay long in any one place.

"Why did I become an actress?" I asked myself. In these circumstances my profession became my enemy, but there was nothing I could do about it now.

Whenever I moved into another in-law's home, the neighbors started to talk about me, peeping through or looking over the fence. They may have guessed that I was a movie actress and radio commentator. They made unintentionally dangerous remarks out of their curiosity that could easily have led to my detection by puppet collaborators.

In several cases, the homes where I stayed were searched. "I heard the chief of the Seoul radio station came to your house," said one investigator, and he grinned.

One day, when we were hiding in Kuryong village of Puyan, news came from Seoul that pressure was being put on my family to find me. It was then that I made up my mind to return to Seoul at once. A young man, a relative of mine, helped us get forged identification cards, and on August 19 the four of us, Ik-Chin Kim's wife, her daughter, Chinyung and I, left for Seoul.

On the way, in the Chokkong Village of Chongyang District, we were caught by the home guards. When I showed one of them my forged identification card my hand trembled. He must have sensed that it was forged, for he took us to the village police station.

While we were being questioned, our examiners learned that Chief Prosecutor Ik-Chin Kim's family was traveling. When they got this clue they started to treat us very roughly. First they locked us in, then, very late that night, the examination began.

They asked me where Ik-Chin Kim was. I said that he had followed the government to Taegu. But the examiner insisted that everyone else in our party had already confessed where Mr. Kim was hiding and that I should confess too. He said, "The others tell me you know where Ik-Chin Kim is. Don't lie."

He made me so angry I didn't know what to do. All night long he kept trying to make me answer questions, and all night long I refused to answer. I don't think anybody in our party slept that night, for the gloomy shadows were hanging on our faces and our eyes were bloodshot.

On the second night the examination started again.

Ik-Chin Kim's wife and her daughter were questioned first. Then my daughter and I were taken in, but they did not let us stay together. They locked me in a room, and I clenched my fists and bit my lips as they dragged my daughter to another room close by.

I heard a beating sound, then my daughter shrieked. I felt as if my own bones were being crushed.

Then I heard a shot. I knew something was happening to Chinyung. I became unconscious.

When I regained consciousness a home guard was bending over me. He said, "Your daughter has been shot to death. There is no need for you to continue to lie."

I felt as if I were seeing stars. My first impulse was to strike the examiner, but instead I said, "As you please. My daughter is shot to death. Still I have nothing to confess. You'd better shoot me too." Then I got up and told him to take me to the examining room.

I couldn't control my legs. They were very shaky, not from fear, but from anger. Truly I was not afraid of death. Where my daughter went I didn't hesitate to go.

But the examiner was flurried because of my determined attitude. He suddenly softened and said with a smile, "Will you confess if I let your daughter come to you alive?"

I didn't know what to make of this. Then I saw Chinyung being led into the room.

"Chinyung!" I screamed.

"Mother!" she called.

We hugged one another as if we were risen from the dead.

While we were being tortured by the home guards I found a friend among them, a young man with a fair complexion. He told me that he was a Seminary student and had been forced to join the home guard. He must have taken pity on me, for he said to me quietly, "Don't worry. I will see that you are released as soon as possible."

It may have been by his effort that we were freed the next day. When we were leaving I asked his name, but with a cold smile he said, "Never mind. If I get to Seoul alive I will call on you."

I worried for his life and felt sad for him.

On August 28, exhausted in body and mind, we arrived in Seoul. I rushed home immediately but my husband was missing and the hospital was being guarded by puppet soldiers. The cook and the nurses had been chased out, but they had begged and begged and finally had been allowed to keep a small gate room. My daughter and I went into this room and rested.

Four hours after I arrived at home, at nine o'clock that evening, I was taken to the Central Police Station. A friend had informed on me, a young actor whom I had known for ten years and who had treated me like a sister.

After six days I was transferred to the City Security Office. I was released on September 12 after all kinds of tortures, and was ordered to receive special education in propaganda.

The person responsible for my education was a prosecutor from the Supreme Prosecutor's office, a woman called Chin-Hong Pak, wife of the late Tae-Jun Kim. She lectured to me on politics for two hours each time.

September 16! The unforgettable day in my life! On this day the R.O.K. army and the U.N. forces landed on Inchon! According to schedule, I had dragged myself to the woman prosecutor and then to the movie actors' alliance office. Strangely enough, the officials said, "You look tired. You'd better go home and take a rest." They seemed very friendly. My health was very bad then. I was nothing but skin and bones. Due to the long distances I had to walk, both of my feet were infected. There is still some humane feeling left in them, I thought, as I stepped out of the office with a sort of gratitude.

When I came out to the road someone was following me. It was a young man who used to work at the Tongdo theatre.

"You'd better escape. It won't be safe to go home," he said quietly.

My heart sank. But quickly I changed my direction and hid myself.

I found out later that two plainclothes policemen were at the house waiting for me.

All those who were arrested at that time were executed.

In-Yung Kim

What Happened to a Clergyman

Pastor Kim is well known in missionary circles in Korea.

On June 27 the ministers from all the churches in Seoul gathered in the Central Church to discuss ways and means of helping the refugees coming into the city. It was evening when the meeting ended and I returned home. By this time, the noise of the big guns had so unnerved and frightened my family that I thought it best to take them to a place of safety. We went to the nearby home of an American missionary and hid in the basement. It was that night that Seoul became a world of Communist bandits.

I spent the next few days between my home and the missionary's house, shuttling back and forth uneasily. In the meantime the persecution started and my home was investigated. First the home guards came, six or seven of them, each in trousers and jacket, with a straw hat and a red armband, and carrying a gun. They were rude and rough. They searched the whole house very carefully, and when they were through they took away our furniture, not only our own belongings but other things which had been entrusted to us.

During the first weeks of July we held church services as we could. But conditions grew steadily worse and no one knew how long it would take for the R.O.K. army to recapture Seoul.

At the beginning of August, pressure from the Communists increased and it became plain that my life was in danger. At this time a young man whom I knew began calling on me. He was Pum-Yul Lee, who used to come to my church. He asked me to surrender voluntarily and said that if I didn't my property and my life would be destroyed.

"To surrender voluntarily! What sin have I committed that I should surrender?" I gasped, and stared at him, not only surprised by this request but shocked that it should have come from one who used to attend my church. His answer left me in no doubt about his sympathies.

"You have committed no sin? You are pro-American and you are on the side of the Republic of Korea, and yet you say you have no sin?" Then he pointed out things I had done which were now considered crimes by the Communists. He spoke with anger and I answered indignantly. To think that this young man could so persecute me was heart-breaking.

After many uncomfortable days someone came in the night and shook my gate. It was well past midnight.

"Open the gate! Open the gate!" a voice shouted.

The whole family awakened and trembled. They begged me to escape while there was still time. But I made up my mind to entrust the whole thing to God and to obey Him. If He wanted me to die by a Communist's hand I would go to Him with a smile; if He wanted me to live longer for some task yet to do, I would do it gladly.

"Open the gate! Open the gate! Is In-Yung Kim there?" They shook the gate impatiently.

"Yes, I am here," I answered quietly, and opened the gate.

A group of seven or eight puppet bandits with Japanese swords and guns rushed in. "Where is In-Yung Kim?" they demanded.

"I am he," I answered.

"Oh you are!" said one of them. Then he grabbed me and took me out to the yard. He made me stand by the hydrant while another pointed a gun at me.

I closed my eyes tight. I thought the hour had come to go to God. But no shot was fired. Instead, the investigator went into my house.

The small electric organ in our church had a transformer attached. The trouble now was that organ, which I had moved from the church to my house when the disturbance started. The puppet bandits brought the organ out to the yard.

"What is this?" they asked.

"It is an electric organ," I answered.

"We know that, but what is it for?"

"It is used for church services."

"Stop talking nonsense. You think we don't know that? For what else is it being used?"

"No other purpose, I am sure. It is used for the church services. I was afraid it might be lost so I brought it to my home."

"Don't lie! If you do you will be shot to death. We know how well ministers tell a lie."

I gasped—I couldn't speak.

"Isn't short-wave used in connection with this? You are nothing but a spy for the reactionaries, under a well-disguised and beautiful name, Religion," they declared. Then they said that by scientific investigation they had found certain proof of just where the organ was being used.

The puppet bandits dragged me out the gate. Outside

were more than ten other puppet soldiers in readiness. It was a frightening sight.

I was taken straight to the Political Security Office in the West Gate Police Station and for three days I was subjected to all kinds of torture. But no matter how they examined the organ they could not find any short-wave used in connection with it. Finally I was released. My family were all crying when they saw me, for they had thought they would never see me again in this world.

I thought so, too.

From the day I was released I led a hidden life. First I hid in the basement of the missionary's house, but after ten days I had to move out because the puppet soldiers were using the house. Next I hid under the church chimney and sometimes I went into the storeroom in our yard and covered myself with a straw mat. The storeroom was like a basement, with a lot of shrubs planted on top of it. Perhaps I was safe because I hid myself in such surroundings; we have a proverb which says that beneath an oil lamp is the darkest place.

Our home was next to the church, which was used as an educational center for wounded puppet soldiers. My anger and indignation were indescribable when I saw it all while hiding in their midst.

One night about one o'clock I decided to go out. First I listened at the storeroom door. No one seemed to be there. I opened the door and peeped out. My breath almost stopped when I saw a puppet soldier sitting on a stone holding a burp gun. He must have been a sentry. Fortunately, he was facing the church and I saw only his back. I closed the door very gently, but I must have been overcautious, for it squeaked.

The puppet soldier got up suddenly and said, "What's

that?" A chill went down my back and I stood up stiff and straight behind the door.

The puppet soldier looked around, then walked toward the main gate. He must have been afraid of being alone, because he called a comrade.

"Comrade X! Comrade X!" he shouted, and I heard someone answering him. Then the first soldier spoke again. "Come quick! I heard something in the shrubs. Let's investigate it."

"Investigate for what?" asked the second. "It's only a squirrel. Lots of squirrels in the shrubs." He may have been afraid to investigate, and was probably tired.

When his comrade failed to respond, the sentry went to another place. But even after he had gone I couldn't sleep. I stayed awake all that night.

The next day I hid myself in the belfrey, climbing up the bell tower when no one was around. The belfrey was very dusty and there were many cobwebs. I lay down and saw the U.N. planes flying over, and I offered my prayers for the quick recapture of Seoul by the U.N. forces and the Republic army.

Indeed, God did hear our prayers—Seoul was recaptured soon after that. From the belfrey where I lay it rings out, *ding, dong, ding,* the sacred peal of the bell.

Soon-Chun Pak

What Happened to a Congresswoman

Soon-Chun Pak is generally thought to be one of Korea's most prominent and influential women.

I learned of the invasion of the Communist bandits when a woman police officer brought me the news early in the morning of June 25th.

At 2:15 A.M. on June 27th, my phone rang and I received a message to come at once to the National Assembly. I was not so sure that the message was authentic, so I rang up Mr. Iky Shin, who assured me that there was an emergency call for the National Assembly. At 3:15 A.M. I reached the Capitol and found 104 members present.

Speaker Iky Chin said, "Both the government and the army have decided to move and the National Assembly has been asked to move with them. I cannot make the decision alone. That is why the Assembly is called." After much debate and discussion we decided to stay in Seoul to the last. When I left the Capitol the sun had risen, and I could hear the battle being fought in Miari.

At that time the Korean Women's Society was holding a meeting of district representatives. There were twenty or more representatives in Seoul. I advised them to cross the Han River as quickly as possible. Then I walked about aimlessly all day long, unable to lose the empty feeling in my heart.

The streets were heavily crowded by refugees already. The farmers dropped their work and came to the city, some pulling cows and oxen and some riding in oxcarts.

I was saddened all day by the sight of crowds of refugees, and I wept until my eyes were red and swollen.

At four o'clock that afternoon I went to the Korean Women's Society office and saw two representatives still there. Angrily I said to them, "Didn't I tell you to cross the Han River as quickly as possible?"

"What are you going to do, President?" they asked me.

"I am going to stay here. The National Assembly has decided not to leave Seoul until it is besieged." Thus answering I sent the two women across the Han River.

Toward evening on that day the sound of big guns from the north grew louder, minute by minute. I went out to the street again and started to walk around. Walking helped me to calm down a little. I stopped at the Women's Daily News Building and found the staff dissolved and the building closed. I was disgusted with their behavior because they had gone without letting the president know.

I went to the Seoul station and watched the confused and perplexed refugees there. Later at a friend's house near-by I found the members of the directorate of the Korean Leather Company. They were to have crossed the Han River in a car but the bridge was already blown up when they got there so they had returned. I stayed up all night with them.

Throughout the night we kept telephoning reporters and investigators of the Capitol. Minute by minute, conditions grew worse. But suddenly good news came. The SCAP Operation Mission was established in Youngdunpo and a hundred planes had arrived. Just for a few minutes we forgot our troubles and drank to the SCAP operation. Then at daybreak we rang up again, but the connections were cut off and there was no answer.

At six in the morning I sent a man out for news. He returned and said that the R.O.K. army had retreated. I sent a man out again at eight o'clock. He came back with the news that the puppet army tanks had reached the Seoul station. Overnight, the world had turned upside-down.

At noon I went out disguised in a long skirt and a waist and wearing a turban-like white scarf on my head. Through back roads and alleys I arrived in Susong-Dong and from there went to Jaedong.

With two friends, Sung-Ho Pak and Yei-Hang Lee, I hid there until July 2nd. My friends left on that day and on the next, July 3rd, I was arrested by a Communist bandit while I was hiding in the attic. Someone must have informed on me, for the Communist came into the house, walked straight to the attic and opened the door as if it were his own house.

He smiled and said, "How have you been?" and offered his hand. He looked like a big boy.

I said, "Who are you?"

"I am from the Northern half of Korea."

"Have you an identification card?"

He showed it to me and I saw that he was a political security officer.

"Who do you think I am?" I asked.

He grinned and answered, "I saw your photograph while I was in the Northern half of Korea and I know very well who you are."

He then took me to the Chongno police station. When we entered the station he walked ahead of me and I followed about five yards behind him. People must have seen this and thought I was going in to surrender voluntarily. The puppet rabble propagandized through posters and rumors that I had made a voluntary surrender.

That night in the cell I tried to commit suicide by tying my stockings around my neck. But at the point of tightening the hose around my throat I thought of my children: "How could a mother of seven do away with herself?" I put the stockings down.

At eleven the second night, I was taken out into the back yard of the police station. At that moment I realized that what I had been expecting had come. I felt as calm as a quiet lake. I had had one creed to live by: to live a pure life and to die with a smile.

But to my surprise, instead of being shot I was taken into a room and questioned. They asked how many were in my family and how many kans [1 kan = 36 sq. ft.] in my house. After a brief hearing they released me and I came home.

About an hour later I was taken in again, this time to the police station chief's office. The chief was a young man.

"Teacher Pak, how are you?" he welcomed me politely. I sat across the desk from the chief with a Stalin statuette on the desk between us.

The chief asked me of my thoughts and feelings. I answered that I didn't have any.

"But do you think the invasion was started by the North or was it the South?" he queried.

"I am a citizen of the Republic of Korea and I believe in the statement made by the government of the Republic of Korea," I answered proudly.

He said, "No, the South started the invasion," and then he grinned. "I came to Seoul as a Partisan three months ago and I know of your political views. They are not much different from ours. Why do you work for the rightists? Come to us. You have committed much sin with your activities. The only way for you to get a pardon is to change your allegiance to the People's Republic and work for it."

"If I have sinned," I told him, "it is because I am ambitious for my country and because I love my people. If a statesman is for the Republic of Korea one day and for the People's Republic the next, he never can get the support of the people, and if he cannot get support he is out as a statesman. No matter what, I only love and care for our flag which is the symbol of our people. When I was twelve, at the time when Japan annexed Korea, I saw with my own eyes my father burying the flag in an earthen jar. Then during the Independence Movement, with the flag in my hand I called 'Ten thousand years for Korea!' in front of the Japanese police officers' bayonets, until my throat gave out. To such a flag how can I stop my allegiance?"

At this point the chief of the police station, pacing the floor with his arms folded, sighed and said to me, "You have dreamed a long dream. You'd better think it over."

On July 8th I was transferred to the Political Security Office. On the 13th, six of us were released when a group of people came from the North especially to re-educate the National Assembly members.

From that day on, I escaped arrest not so much by my own efforts as through fate.

On September 17th, when many signs pointed to the early recapture of Seoul, I went to Mr. Sang-Kyu Paik's house to discuss the situation. Also there was Mr. Sei-

Hun Won. I suggested that we leave the city, for it was necessary to escape the last violence of the Communist bandits. We were all of the same opinion. Mr. Sei-Hun Won went to advise Dr. Kyu-Sik Kim to leave. Soon after he had gone someone knocked on the gate. We were told that the man wanted to survey the house.

"Why would anyone come to survey a house at a time like this? It is a trick to get in. Let us escape," I said.

Mr. Paik went to his next-door neighbor's and I left the house by another way. He was arrested that night in his neighbor's house. I went directly to the house of the late Yun-Meng Sun's wife and hid there. It was a handy place to hide because she had four houses on the same lot and all were connected with one another. But on September 25th the house was completely demolished in an air raid. Miraculously, nothing happened to me.

I took a wounded person on my back to a student's home near the Paichai school in Sosomun. Then, covering myself with the blood-stained skirt of the wounded, I went on to Jaedong. On the way I was examined seven times. Each time I acted as if I were wounded.

In Jaedong I went to a friend's house and spent the night. In the morning I climbed up to the attic and looked toward Anguk-Dong. I saw the flag flying at the Emun Building and U.N. tanks passing by. I had no feeling. I was like a stone or a block of wood.

Seoul was recaptured but there was no news from the numerous friends who had been arrested. Now I have only two wishes: one, I don't want to be born again as a Korean after I die, and the other, I don't want to live any longer.

Epilogue

One of the current jokes in Seoul after the occupation was to the effect that it was hard to find a Communist while he was still warm. And the relative accuracy of this apparently whimsical observation certainly appeared during the early winter months when the account related in this volume was being pieced together. The atmosphere was an unhealthy one for avowed Communists and sympathizers. Even the most accurate sampling of public opinion (if such could have been obtained under the circumstances) would not have revealed many Communists in South Korea—they were neither available, nor were they talking. In fact, it will probably never be known in precise terms how many converts the Communists made during their three months of occupation.

One clue, however, to an understanding of the impact of Communism in Korea is at hand. When the tide of battle suddenly turned late in November, 1950, and the reoccupation of Seoul by the Communists appeared imminent, Gen. Matthew B. Ridgeway, then Commander of the U.S. Eighth Army was prompted to observe that "The southward exodus of several million refugees before the oncoming Communist flood presents perhaps the greatest tragedy to which Asia has ever been subjected in the course of its long history." While the mid-winter spectacle of these refugees, overcrowding every vehicle from oxcart to railroad flatcar, filling the roads with travelers on foot—the men with overloaded A-frames and the women with overwhelming head loads and babies on their backs papoose style—could be called a tragedy in its own right, the greater tragedy lay in the reasons for this mass movement. The tentacles of Communism were again reaching into South Korea, and a population was again recoiling at the prospect. Nor were the South Koreans the only ones who were forsaking their homes. For a few weeks during October and November the U.N. forces had liberated a good part of North Korea and when, early in the winter, the course of events changed, North Koreans also started the long trek south. How many hundreds of thousands started southward, and how many survived the ordeals of the journey will never be known. But the stark fact remains that large masses of people were reacting to Communism by sacrificing their possessions, uprooting their families, and exposing themselves to untold and unknown hardships, in return for the possibility of escape from the system.

While this tragic migratory population can scarcely be thought representative of Korea as a whole, a study* of their motives for becoming refugees and the intensity of their anti-Communist feelings offers some limited perspectives upon the attempted sovietization of Korea.

There are striking differences (Chart I) between the North and South Korean refugees in their expressed reasons for fleeing from Communism; five years under tyranny is a far cry from three months. Three-fourths of the North Koreans voiced reasons which may directly be ascribed to the operation of the Communist system —marked for retaliation, restrictions on freedom—in con-

*See the article "Flight from Communism," by the present authors and the writer of the Foreword to this volume, in *Public Opinion Quarterly*, Summer Issue 1951.

trast to about half of the South Koreans. It is, perhaps, of more than passing interest that in both cases the ideological repugnance to Communism in terms of the loss of freedom of speech and movement runs a poor second to the more impelling consideration that the system has "marked" a member of the family by virtue of anti-Communist sentiment or action.

But whatever the precise distribution of reasons may have been for the hundreds of thousands who actually became refugees, it is clear that it is inherent in the Communist system to tolerate neither defectors nor criticism. Possibly the differences between the North and South are smaller than would have been logically expected. That as many as four out of ten South Korean refugees had experienced the bitter lot of being "put on a list" after only three months of the system, is perhaps significant. At the same time it is undoubtedly no accident that nearly twice as many North Koreans found the restrictions intolerable, although the slightly higher ratio of "marked" northerners simply constitutes one further bit of evidence that the Communists put first things first. The rapid elimination of their enemies is a prerequisite to the introduction of the bulk of their "reforms" and far-reaching restrictions.

What course of action these refugees felt they would have followed if they had been unable to flee may roughly be interpreted as a measure of the strength of their anti-Communist feeling, and in their opinions on this point there are again marked differences between the North and South Korean refugees (Chart II). Among the North Koreans, half reported that they would have taken aggressive action by going underground and fight-

Chart 1. REASONS FOR FLEEING

		% North Koreans	% South Koreans
Marked for retaliation	Some member of family is "marked" because of anti-Communist sentiment or action	34	20
	A family member is in ROK army or police	20	21
		54	**41**
Restrictions on freedom	Forced labor, lack of freedom	10	6
	Taxes, forced contributions, etc.	4	2
	Fear of conscription in NK army	6	4
		20	**12**
Reasons not directly related to Communism	Fear of being in war area	6	10
	Advised by local authorities to move	13	26
	Moved along with friends and neighbors	4	6
	Fear of Chinese	3	5
	Other	*	*
		26	**47**
		100%	**100%**
	*Less than ½ of one percent	(=462)	(=857)

North Koreans *South Koreans*

54%

41%

20%

12%

26%

47%

CHART 2. ALTERNATIVES TO FLEEING FROM

	% North Koreans	% South Koreans
Would have gone underground and fought against Communism	49	27
Would have hidden out	37	49
Would have tried to cooperate with Communists	11	17
Don't know what we would have done	3	7
Other	*	*
	100%	100%
	(=462)	(=857)

*Less than ½ of one percent

COMMUNISM (Indicating Strength of Anti-Communist Feeling)

North Koreans

49%

37%

11%

South Koreans

27%

49%

17%

ing. In contrast, only slightly over one-fourth of the South Koreans indicate that they would have been so motivated; and half of them reported that they probably would have attempted to hide out. The conclusion, then, is clear. People who have had experience with Communism for a matter of years rather than months are apt to feel more intensely about it and to take more aggressive action.

Such, in brief, is the statistical story of the Korean refugees. It is a consistent story and a reasonably convincing one. Certainly it tends, in every respect, to bear out the judgment of the present writers that the experience of Koreans under Communism was progressively disillusioning and that only small minorities, be they north or south of the 38th parallel, were completely taken in by the stratagem and machinations of the invaders. It also affirms our observation that the Communist system promises much to many but in fact delivers its rewards to only a few. And finally, these statistical fragments provide but another way of looking at a system which can exist only on the basis of monopoly of power and rigid surveillance. The individual, as an independent human being, has no place.

If these observations be even approximately correct, then the free peoples of the world may take heart. But the rejoicing should not be premature. Perhaps the foregoing stories tell more about Communism than several volumes of description and analysis. Confusion, despair, hope, grief, elation, hunger, fear—these are the ingredients.

How many more such accounts must be written?

Index

Index